"This is a gem of a book, thoughtf
relevant in this time of a climate en
change and deepen our spiritual rela

—**WILLIAM WEST**, visiting pro...........University of Chester

"Flowers touch something essential, deep within us, and in sundry ways they move us. Bríd Kennedy's book is a transformative and life-enhancing exploration of the captivating world of flowers. With themes such as love and joy, beauty, scent and color, resilience, gratitude, and awakening, the reader is led into the garden of experience which is burgeoning with all that makes up the mystery of life."

—**DAVID WHITE**, professional horticulturist,
Anglican priest, and trained spiritual director

"Flowering plants represent the pinnacle of evolutionary achievement in the plant world: the unfolding of living possibility in which God is experienced. And yet the significance of this is a theme that has never been explored in any depth in accounts of modern creation spirituality. Bríd Kennedy's book is a pioneering work in this regard, opening a door on a world of beauty and complexity that enriches both spirituality and theology, and opens new possibilities for how we care for the earth and for the development of a new ecumenism."

—**JOHN FEEHAN**, botanist and geologist

"This beautiful book stands at the vanguard of the emerging literature on the spirituality of flowers. The importance of nature to our spiritual lives is well known, but not the unique gifts that flowers offer to our healing and to our spiritual development. Bríd Kennedy brings the reader on a rich and colorful journey through diverse aspects of the ancient relationship between humans and the floral universe. She touches on the aesthetic, artistic, medicinal, somatic, and religious qualities of flower wisdom and brings it all together to present the spiritual benefit to humans when we are present to flowers in a contemplative way. Writing from her personal experience of the healing benefits of being with the flowers in her garden during COVID-19, and grounded in fascinating academic research, Kennedy demonstrates how her contemplative relationship with flowers supported her inner journey of human-Divine transformation, and how flowers can support our awakening too. This book is a joy to read—full of light, color, and wisdom that brings floral healing to body and soul, and most importantly, to the heart. A reading experience that evokes the joy of being in a field of wildflowers on a summer's day."

—AEDAMAR KIRRANE, author of *Light on Fire: Waking Up to Divine Love*

"At a time of climate change, where we witness the damaging effects of human intervention on the earth, this book reminds us of the interconnectedness and sacredness of the universe of which flowers and humans are a part. It helps us to appreciate the spirituality of the 'ordinary' or the 'mundane.' Using a methodology of authentic subjectivity, Bríd engages on a spiritual journey of meaning-making, connection, and transformation while studying the Divine-human transformational process of flower appreciation. In doing so, she takes the reader on a similar journey of appreciation of the spirituality of flowers."

—CLAUDIA PSAILA, senior lecturer, psychologist, and social worker, University of Malta

Spirituality of Flowers

Spirituality of Flowers

What Flowers Do for Us

BRÍD KENNEDY

Foreword by Niamh Brennan

WIPF & STOCK · Eugene, Oregon

SPIRITUALITY OF FLOWERS
What Flowers Do for Us

Wipf & Stock
An Imprint of Wipf and Stock Publishers
199 W. 8th Ave., Suite 3
Eugene, OR 97401

www.wipfandstock.com

PAPERBACK ISBN: 979-8-3852-2678-8
HARDCOVER ISBN: 979-8-3852-2679-5
EBOOK ISBN: 979-8-3852-2680-1

VERSION NUMBER 10/22/24

Contents

Foreword

IN THE PAST CENTURY, as we have learned more about the evolution of the universe and our own blue-green planet within it, there has been a movement from understanding our world as an inanimate object to an earth that is alive and interconnected. Paleontologist and Jesuit priest Pierre Teilhard de Chardin[1] took us some way into this change of view. Through scientific study and insight we were gradually being called to a shift in our understanding from the nature of reality as being in a static state to one of continuous emergence, a time-developmental universe. This is referred to as "cosmogenesis." For Teilhard, a universe in "cosmogenesis" integrated in a convincing way his intuitive love of matter with his intrinsic recognition of spirit. In this process, spirit and matter could now be seen to be two aspects of the same reality. Passionist priest and cultural historian Thomas Berry took us still further in this understanding. As early as 1979 he wrote an essay titled "The Spirituality of the Earth."[2] In the essay, he argues how a spirituality of earth refers to a quality of earth itself, not just a human quality. Furthermore, if there is no spirituality in earth, then there is no spirituality in the human. At its core, he states, our spirituality is earth-derived.

Since then, the spirituality of the earth and our participation in it has come to be increasingly considered in philosophy,

1. Teilhard de Chardin, *Human Phenomenon*, 154.
2. Berry, "Contemporary Spirituality."

vii

theology, spirituality, and ecology. The connection between our soul and the soul of the world and the implications of our separation and denial of this aspect of reality, not just for earth and all those we share earth with, but also for our human selves, is forming a growing pool of ecological thinking. This was evidenced strongly in Pope Francis's encyclical on the environment, *Praise Be to You—Laudato Si'*,[3] when he stated that the root causes of our environmental crisis are spiritual and ethical.

In this unique and wonderfully layered book, Bríd Kennedy takes us further into this understanding. Drawing on science, spirituality studies, evolutionary development, and related literature, she limits her lens to focus exclusively on the spirituality of flowers. Her question is whether flower appreciation (the seemingly most natural thing in the world) is, in fact, participation in a Divine-human transformation process, and in this beautiful book, Kennedy walks with us toward an answer.

This book is a fascinating blend that highlights the significance of flowers and their interconnectedness within the complex systems of earth. Kennedy deliberately draws out the influence of flowers upon us spiritually, aesthetically, and physically. For example, not only do certain species of flower contain anti-oxidants and anti-inflammatories but studies have also shown that flowers may visually stimulate the brain, and the symmetry in their shape contributes to our making sense of the world. Perhaps most noticeable is the sensory effect that flowers can have on us—their scent, their color, their form—and Kennedy takes us still deeper into this understanding through using science to illustrate all of life's essential connectedness. At the heart of this is the effect of paying attention to the flower on our affective and spiritual dimension. In some way always instinctively known, but here explained.

Hers is a mystagogical approach, a tentative touch with mystery. More an invitation than a declaration. She is calling us to look and to look again. Beauty, she writes, and our ability to appreciate it is at the heart of the spiritual journey. This has echoes of the

3. Francis, *Praise Be to You*, 12.

work of Brian Swimme and Mary Evelyn Tucker[4] who claim it is our ability to wonder that will save us. And wonder Kennedy does, her own questions and curiosity inviting the same in the reader. Kennedy implicates herself in the research through a practice of authentic interiority "striving toward beauty, intelligibility, truth, goodness, and love" (p. 22). In the book she illustrates through her own experience and other researched literature how an appreciation of flowers can create and orient this experience. This is an interchange of the sacred between us, the ability to recognize, honor, and most significantly, be moved by the sacred within another—an other than human—and more still to recognize the effect that has on oneself. Through reading, reflection, and journaling on her own experience Kennedy not only presents an homage to flowers, an essential part of creation, but comes to realize how "the well-being of our body is not possible without the well-being of our planet and that is why, to protect the well-being of our body, we must protect the planet" (p. 22).

Many decades ago, Rachel Carson advised that "those who contemplate the beauty of the earth find reserves of strength that will endure as long as life lasts."[5] Such was Carson's insight that an entire environmental movement has been established around this premise. This is to respond to our critical ecological crisis not from a place of fear but from a place of love. From the knowledge of the interconnectedness of all beings with each other, the realization that our own human well-being is intrinsically and infinitely linked to the well-being of our earth. To contemplate earth's beauty and to love our planet back to health.

And so welcome to Bríd Kennedy's book which brings us another step closer to falling in love. It couldn't have come at a more urgent time.

Niamh Brennan, PhD
South East Technological University, Ireland
July 2024

4. Swimme and Tucker, *Journey to the Universe*.
5. Carson, *Silent Spring*, 34.

Acknowledgments

I SINCERELY THANK EVERYONE involved in running the Masters in Applied Spirituality program. I deeply enjoyed every moment of this powerful and amazing program through the thought-provoking subjects presented with warmth, stirring deep curiosity by Bernadette Flanagan, Noelia Molina, Michael O'Sullivan and all other tutors. The sacred listening spaces and often-challenging assignments led me on an inspiring and enriching soul journey reconnecting me with my spirit and that of the universe.

Special thanks to Bernadette Flanagan for helping me identify my thesis topic, which has brought me on an inspiring journey. I deeply appreciate all the encouragement and affirmation that Noelia has given me throughout the program and as my thesis supervisor. Her affirmation, clarity of guidance, patience, and wisdom is just Beautiful.

I will forever treasure all my class colleagues for their heartfelt discussions, soul-sharing, sense of humor, honesty, love, inspiration, friendship, support, and joy.

I extend my special thanks to Kathleen our librarian, who always warmly welcomed me to the library and promptly and professionally assisted me in every way to access relevant literature.

Finally, I sincerely thank my husband, son, daughter, and friends for all your kindness, encouragement, support, patience, and guidance, which I deeply value and treasure.

Abstract

AS A CHILD, I was fascinated with the beautiful scents and shapes of flowers such as primroses, daffodils, and lilacs. It stirred something deep within me that I could not name. During COVID-19 lockdowns, I recognized the joy, peace, and healing I received from seeing flowers of all shapes, smells, and colors grow and blossom.

The mystery and beauty of flowers stirred my curiosity to develop my research question: Is flower appreciation a participation in a Divine-human transformation process and, if so, how is it being expressed? My practice of authentic interiority, which is mystagogical, led me to the mysterious meaning of myself and four selected authors of books relating to the spiritual experiences of flowers. The authenticity of the lived experience, of my selected four authors, and myself was self-implicating of existing in our subjectivity in a state of dynamic orientation toward beauty, intelligibility, truth, goodness, and love indicating that we had immanent experiences of the Transcendent.

Now, more than ever, I realize how interdependent we humans are on all creation. Flowers are an essential part of creation bringing in wisdom and healing. Appreciating them is a participation in a Divine-human transformation process expressed through our acknowledgment of the scent, color, shape, and any changes in these through our deep knowing that something sacred is within them. Taking precious moments to stand and smell flowers

Abstract

enriches our souls as it reminds us of who we are as humans and to care for Mother Earth.

"Recognizing my Beauty is deep within"
—Bríd Kennedy, 2023

Introduction

"Every flower is a soul blossoming in nature"
—GÉRARD DE NERVAL, 1854

AS A CHILD, I was fascinated with the beautiful scents and shapes of flowers such as primroses, daffodils, and lilacs. It stirred something deep within me that I could not name. I learned about nature while growing up on a farm as I experienced the cycle of life, through the new growth and harvest of crops, and appreciating "God's Garden," which grows wildflowers such as daisies, dandelions, and buttercups.

I now reflect on my lived experience since my childhood to make sense of our world. My career spanning four decades, witnessing poverty and gender-based violence amid the destruction of soil, forests, water, and air, with more frequent famines, floods, and conflicts has led me to believe that an "impoverishment of the soul" exists.[6] During COVID-19 lockdowns, I found working directly with the soil in my garden, growing wild and cultivated flowers—talking to them and seeing some as if responding to me, blooming beautifully—spiritually nourishing and stirring all my senses.

6. Fox, *Creation Spirituality*, xiii.

When writing my spiritual autobiography, I recognized the great joy, peace, and healing I receive from seeing flowers of all shapes, smells, and colors grow and blossom. Over time, many children and adults have shared the joy they experience from flowers with me. COVID-19 lockdowns were the first time that I had the opportunity to spend quality time in my garden, which proved therapeutic as I shared various miraculous, magical, and mystical experiences of flower growth and blossoming with my family and friends.

I am now realizing through my studies in the Masters in Applied Spirituality program, that our souls are one with nature. I am concerned with the global ecological crisis and the need to protect Mother Earth. This research is set in a context where climate change is seriously risking the survival of humanity and nature. We live in a globalized, increasingly secular, complex world where the COVID-19 pandemic has led many people to reflect on their lifestyles and where others have chosen destructive pathways. More and more people are looking within and opting for a contemplative life in nature to live fulfilled and meaningful lives and in doing so, are contributing to global consciousness in striving to end suffering at every level and restore Mother Earth through mindfulness, equality, and climate-change movements across the globe.[7]

The mystery and beauty of flowers emerged as I worked through my program. As awakening happens within at the individual level, and given we are all interconnected, the direct and primordial experience of being part of nature's omnipresent, cyclic course has led me to delve deeper to understand what is happening within me.

This led me to explore if and what spiritual transformation happens when engaging with gardening and with flowers, and the impact it has on human emotions such as forgiveness, letting go, trusting, and love. As I began my research, I found lots of literature related to the spirituality of gardening but the question remained for me, What is it about flowers that bring us joy? This curiosity led me to develop my research question: Is flower appreciation a

7. Hollick and Connelly, *Hope for Humanity*, 21–44.

participation in a Divine-human transformation process and, if so, how is it being expressed?

My thesis invites the reader on the Divine-human transformation journey through the process of flower appreciation. In chapter 1, I present the history and influence of flowers on humans. Understanding spirituality is outlined in chapter 2. Exploring flower appreciation is described in chapter 3. The joy, beauty, scent, color, and resilience are presented in chapter 4.

Chapter One

History and Influence of Flowers on Humans

1. Introduction

SINCE ANCIENT TIMES PEOPLE across all cultures have had a huge attraction to flowers, using them as a medium to express sentiments of goodwill, love, beauty, and sadness, with each flower having different meanings individually and globally.

Botanists call flowering plants angiosperms. These provide us and the animal world with nourishment that is fundamental to our existence. I will briefly explain the origin of flowers and their influence over millennia, predominantly focusing on the impact that wild and cultivated flowers have on people's spirituality, creativity, and well-being.

I will try to establish what is in the expression of this relationship between people and flowers. I will assess how flowers align with the soul, whether a Divine-human transformation occurs, and, if so, how. I will summarize my findings in the conclusion.

2. History and Intelligence of Flower Creation

Flowers began changing the world almost as soon as they appeared on earth about 130 million years ago. Once they took firm root about 30 million years later, they swiftly diversified in an explosion of varieties that established most of the flowering plant families of the modern world[1] playing an essential part in the evolution of human consciousness.[2]

Flowers make up ninety percent of land plant species[3] and are one of the most essential components of life on earth.[4] Botanically, a flower is simply the sexual organ of a plant.[5] Their ability to seed, live, reproduce, and die in short life cycles has allowed them to evolve faster than their competitors, triggering whole new generations[6] which possibly helped give rise to their diversity.[7] Nature shows us that sexual relationship is an integral part of life's expression on earth.[8] Whether a common daisy or a rare and structurally complex orchid, all flowering plants invest a great deal in producing colorful and carefully designed flowers.[9] Once a flower is fertilized, petals are no longer needed.[10]

Nature's intelligence is intuitive, holistic, and nourishing and functions effortlessly and spontaneously.[11] The diversity of flowers is astounding, varying in shape, color, size, scent, and the way they interact with their pollinators. From an evolutionary perspective, the flower as a species uses its aesthetic characteristics to attract humans, a strategy of activating humans to grow and propagate it,

1. Klesius, "Big Bloom," 102–21.
2. Tolle, *New Earth*, 2.
3. Nadot and Carrive, "Colourful Life of Flowers," 120–30.
4. Murray, *Wild Embrace*, 99.
5. Redwood, *Art of Mindful Gardening*, 58.
6. Redwood, *Art of Mindful Gardening*, 58.
7. Stuart-Smith, *Well Gardened Mind*, 138.
8. Newell, *Sacred Earth*, 25.
9. Murray, *Wild Embrace*, 100.
10. Murray, *Wild Embrace*, 102.
11. Chopra, *Seven Spiritual Laws*, 54.

just as it activates insects with pollen.[12] Flowers are living organisms and are part of the earth's complex chain of natural life.[13]

The oxygen in every breath we take, essential for the functioning of every part of our body, comes from plants growing both on land and in the sea.[14] A flower is energy and information; the only difference between the flower and I is our respective bodies' informational and energy content.[15] The energy flowers emit comes from their color and essence giving off distinct vibrations of sound and light.[16] Plants have wisdom to share and by joining in a relationship with them, merging our spirit with the plant's spirit, the strength of the plant's core essence is found and revered.[17]

Humans have always been attracted to flowers,[18] which have been part of many cultures since ancient times.[19] Flowers remain rooted, making themselves very noticeable to us humans as well as to pollinators and animals.[20] We nurture them in our gardens, collect and arrange them in vases, and give them to friends and family in the form of bouquets, indicating their deep significance and symbolism for us.[21] Each plant has special abilities and talents contributing enormously to human wellness.[22] Each plant makes varied contributions to its environment, to animals, to humans, and to other plants by providing oxygen, food, and medicines.[23]

12. Mendelson, *Rhapsody in Green*, 103.

13. Nishi, *Zen Flowers*, 82.

14. Murray, *Wild Embrace*, 106.

15. Chopra, *Seven Spiritual Laws*, 67–68.

16. Pallasdowney, *Voices of Flowers*, 3.

17. Pallasdowney, *Voices of Flowers*, 3.

18. Huss et al., "Humans' Relationship to Flowers," 32.

19. Nishi, *Zen Flowers*, 22.

20. Murray, *Wild Embrace*, 99.

21. Murray, *Wild Embrace*, 82.

22. Costanzo, *Twelve Gifts*, 180.

23. Costanzo, *Twelve Gifts*, 181.

3. Influence of Flowers on Humans

3.1. Spiritual Influence

The central symbolism of Buddhism is the lotus flower, a symbol of purity. A closed bud represents a time before enlightenment, and as the flower gradually opens with its middle still hidden, it indicates enlightenment beyond ordinary sight.[24]

People use flowers as an offering to the gods in the main Hindu prayer rite *puja*, meaning the flower act, in the belief that the fragrance of the flowers pleases the deity, who then grants good health, wealth, and prosperity.[25] The rose is considered to be Lord Krishna's favorite flower while in Judaism it is a metaphor for God's love for the people.[26] Flowers present the subtle and potent relevance of thirty flowering plants in Chinese Daoist culture.[27]

In Christianity, Jesus said, "Consider the lilies, how they grow: they neither toil nor spin" (Luke 12:27 NRSV), "For all flesh is like grass and all its glory like the flower of grass. The grass withers, and the flower falls, but the word of the Lord endures forever" (1 Pet 1:24–25 NRSV). Jesus says if God clothes simple flowers in such beauty, how much more will God clothe you?[28] Plants symbolizing the Virgin Mary include a white lily for her purity, a red rose for her perfect love and the part she played in Christ's passion, violets growing low on the ground symbolize her humility, and the gentle lily of the valley, her meekness.[29] St. Therese of Lisieux saw herself as "The Little Flower of Jesus" because she was like the simple wild flowers—unnoticed, yet growing and praising God.[30]

---

24. Tolle, *New Earth*, 5.
25. Khan, *Callaloo Nation*, 301.
26. Dobbs, *Secret Language of Flowers*, 70.
27. Zhang, *Flowers in Chinese Culture*, 4.
28. Tolle, *New Earth*, 268.
29. Naydler, *Gardening as a Sacred Art*, 36.
30. Beevers, *St. Therese the Little Flower*.

Buddha and Jesus were humanity's early flowers.[31] Sadly, their flowering is not yet possible as their message has largely become distorted and misunderstood.[32]

3.2. Artists, Poets, and Writers

Flowers play a huge part in our folklore and history.[33] Humans' affinity and fascination with flowers are attributed to their ethereal quality[34] sought by artists, poets, and everyday people in search of inspiration, solace, or the simple pleasure of beholding a blossom.[35] Myths, folklore, and cultural associations with flowers date back to Greek, Roman, ancient Chinese, and Native American mythology; others were acquired during the Middle Ages, a rich period for European folklore.[36] Humans have embodied flowers for their aesthetic qualities as demonstrated by stone drawings of flowers found in ancient Egyptian graves 120 thousand years ago, used in festivals during Roman times, and created in silk two thousand years ago in China.[37] Throughout time, flowers were carved into wood, marble, and plaster, woven into tapestry, and used to decorate buildings.[38]

Claude Monet owed becoming a painter to flowers[39] and Vincent van Gogh used the image of sunflowers for much of his artwork.[40] Monet was fascinated with the color and form of the iris while van Gogh found that painting the individual shape of iris flowers calmed him.[41] Many great poets used the poetry of flowers

31. Tolle, *New Earth*, 6.
32. Tolle, *New Earth*, 6.
33. Redwood, *Art of Mindful Gardening*, 57.
34. Tolle, *New Earth*, 4.
35. Klesius, "Big Bloom," 102–21.
36. Dobbs, *Secret Language of Flowers*, 9.
37. Haviland-Jones et al., "Environmental Approach," 104–32.
38. Miller, "Power of Flowers."
39. Masset, *Why We Garden*, 2.
40. Bailey, *Sunflowers Are Mine*, 33.
41. Dobbs, *Secret Language of Flowers*, 76.

to express life—for example, William Wordsworth's *Poetry on Flowers*[42] and *The Blue Iris* by Mary Oliver.[43] William Shakespeare made many references to flowers in his writings.[44] Numerous songs are written about flowers—for example, "Bring Flowers of the Rarest" and many others.[45] Sigmund Freud had a great love of flowers and their natural beauty fed his creative energies.[46] Films—for example, *The Wizard of Oz* and *Beauty and the Beast*—owe much of their success to the narrative influence of flowers that have played a critical role in some of cinema's most memorable moments.[47]

Leonardo da Vinci made detailed diagrams of the anatomical arrangements of flowers, including the pentagonal geometry of the five-petalled violet.[48] Galileo Galilei, often described as the father of modern science, was a keen observer of patterns in nature, from the movement of celestial bodies to the geometry of flowers.[49] Critchlow describes the flower as a teacher of symmetry and geometry.[50] Flowers can be treated as sources of remembering, a way of recalling our wholeness, as well as awakening our inner power of recognition and consciousness.[51] What is evident in the geometry of the face of a flower can remind us of the geometry that underlies all existence.[52]

42. Wordsworth, *Book of Flowers*.

43. Oliver, *Blue Iris*.

44. Kerr, *Shakespeare's Flowers*.

45. Fenton, "35 Best Songs about Flowers."

46. Stuart-Smith, *Well Gardened Mind*, 137.

47. "Flowers in Cinema."

48. Murray, *Wild Embrace*, 106.

49. Murray, *Wild Embrace*, 106.

50. Critchlow, *Hidden Geometry of Flowers*, 8–18.

51. Critchlow, *Hidden Geometry of Flowers*, 8–18.

52. Critchlow, *Hidden Geometry of Flowers*, 8–18.

3.3. Means of Spiritual Communication

Flowers used since pagan times for celebrations and rituals[53] have held special significance for the human spirit.[54] There is evidence that the Neanderthals buried their dead with flowers.[55] Flowers are used to convey sympathy, contrition, romance, or celebration such as pride and joy.[56] People use flowers to express religious feelings and, in some religions, flowers are considered the direct route for spiritual communication.[57]

Flowers can say things that we can't, triggering an emotion or changing behavior.[58] In Victorian England, when many verbal expressions of emotions were suppressed, floriography and floral dictionaries were developed by Lady Mary Wortley Montagu to send coded messages to the receiver.[59] Examples of coded messages include: snowdrops meant hope and purity,[60] lilac was associated with humility,[61] forget-me-knots symbolized personal fidelity,[62] and the red poppy was a symbol of consolation.[63] To give someone a rose was to show admiration for the recipient's beauty or to make an expression of the giver's love, with the appropriate level of affection expressed through the color of the rose.[64] There is no universal floral language.[65]

53. Miller, "Power of Flowers."
54. Tolle, *New Earth*, 4.
55. Solecki, *Shanidar*, 3.
56. Heilmeyer, *Language of Flowers*.
57. Stenta, "From Other Lands," 462–69.
58. Evancic, "Unexpected Meanings of Flowers Revealed."
59. Ferguson, *Old Wives Lore for Gardeners*, 118.
60. Dobbs, *Secret Language of Flowers*, 10.
61. Dobbs, *Secret Language of Flowers*, 68.
62. Dobbs, *Secret Language of Flowers*, 40.
63. Dobbs, *Secret Language of Flowers*, 55.
64. Dobbs, *Secret Language of Flowers*, 82–83.
65. Ferguson, *Old Wives Lore for Gardeners*, 118.

3.4. Mental, Physical, and Spiritual Well-Being

Flowers have a long history of use in traditional medicine. Recordings of the botanicals used in traditional medicine have helped the evolution of modern medicine, which uses plants in a range of drugs.[66] In ancient Ireland, people knew how and where to gather and prepare wild-growing medicinal plants to treat a range of ailments.[67] In the last two hundred years, so many of these skills have begun to disappear from common knowledge.[68]

Twelfth-century mystic Hildegard of Bingen used flowering plants to heal. She said illness is related to suppressed emotions and using our inner wisdom teaches us to open up to the spiritual forces within us. Her model has commonality with traditional Chinese medicine, Islamic medicine, and Ayurveda, the traditional medicine of India.[69]

Many of the health benefits ascribed to eating flowers come from their vitamin and mineral content as well as their antioxidant activity and anti-inflammatory properties.[70] A study in Ecuador with ancestral healers who used a vast variety of medicinal plants found that chamomile was the most frequently used.[71] Homeopathic remedies made from flowers and other plant essences are widely available in the western world,[72] offering simple treatments for physical and emotional issues.

The dandelion is one of the wild Irish flowering foods.[73] Every part of the dandelion can be eaten and they taste pleasantly bitter.[74] Its roots have long been used in herbal medicine as a tonic to clear the liver while its flowers are rich in minerals and have a

---

66. Ahmad et al., *Modern Phytomedicine*, 4.

67. Murray, *Wild Embrace*, 43.

68. Murray, *Wild Embrace*, 44.

69. Strehlow and Hertzka, *Hildergard of Bingen's Medicine*, xii.

70. Zheng et al., "Update on the Health Benefits."

71. Morales et al., "Medicinal Plants," 10–15.

72. Pallasdowney, *Voices of Flowers*, 2.

73. Murray, *Wild Embrace*, 57.

74. Wilson, *Garden for the Senses*, 73.

diuretic effect.[75] In Ireland, elder bushes become laden with bursts of tiny white flowers in June, wafting out their beautiful scent.[76] Their fruits have antiviral properties and are packed with vitamins, boosting the immune system when consumed.[77]

Aura Soma is a revived ancient soul therapy that relies on bottles of dual-colored liquids that incorporate plant extracts, essential oils, and the energies and extracts of precious and semiprecious stones. The energetic properties found in the liquids interact with the individual's aura to help support equilibrium in the body, mind, and spirit.[78]

Flowers are a social equalizer; they touch people and they change their energy regardless of age, demographic, or wealth status, as everyone needs joy and beauty.[79] Flowers are with us at the happiest, most beautiful, and most challenging times in our lives, being magical and healing.[80] Flowers can be sources of remembering, a way of recalling our wholeness, as well as awakening our inner power of recognition and consciousness.[81]

Etty Hillensun, before going to Auschwitz, got peace from meditating on the jasmine and the roses seen from her room.[82] Flowers have immediate and long-term effects on emotional reactions, mood, social behaviors, and even memory for both males and females.[83] Chalmin-Pui et al. found that interventions such as a container of flowering bulbs and annual plants placed outside the front door had a significant effect on the occupant's stress levels, many of whom noted flower color as an important element.[84]

75. Murray, *Wild Embrace*, 57–58.

76. Murray, *Wild Embrace*, 62.

77. Murray, *Wild Embrace*, 63.

78. Wall, *Auro Soma*.

79. Miller, "Power of Flowers."

80. Proust, *From Seed to Bloom*, 1.

81. Critchlow, *Hidden Geometry of Flowers*, 5.

82. Woodhouse, *Etty Hillesum*, 179, 188.

83. Haviland-Jones et al., "Environmental Approach," 104–32; Stuart-Smith, *Well Gardened Mind*, 33.

84. Chalmin-Pui et al., "Why Garden?"

The visual stimulation, together with the ease of recognition and the familiarity engendered by symmetry in flower shapes, may stimulate the brain and be associated with improved mood due to a feeling of being able to make sense of the world.[85] This combined element of familiarity and surprise moves us emotionally, activating both sadness and happiness.[86] Huss et al. surmised that the aesthetic experience of flowers leads to the embodied and socially embedded experience of feeling connected positively to the world.[87] Everything that is in the heavens, on the earth, and under the earth is penetrated with connectedness and penetrated with relatedness.[88]

3.5. Sensory Nature of Flowers

The Celtic tradition had deep gratitude for one another, plants, and the earth. This included gratitude for the gifts of our senses so that we may know one another and the earth, inviting us to re-awaken to and change the way we live, relate, and act.[89] We see the specific, physical characteristics of the flower we engage with and create a personality for each flower. This is considered embodied, as the flower becomes a full body with which to interact through its sensory elements such as smell, shape, and color.[90]

Because of their perfume, shape, and color—in short, because of their beauty—flowers have traditionally served as a common literary device to express human qualities.[91] Tending to and enjoying flowers enables us to interact in a skilled fashion with the environment and to engage with the world.[92] The Buddha said that

85. Ullman et al., "Visual Features," 682–727; Torralba and Oliva, "Statistics," 391–412; O'Callaghan, "Object Perception," 803–29.

86. Haviland-Jones et al., "Environmental Approach," 104–32.

87. Huss et al., "Humans' Relationship," 32.

88. Hildergard of Bingen quoted in Ó Murchú, *Reclaiming Spirituality*, 85.

89. Newell, *Sacred Earth*, 255.

90. Huss et al., "Humans' Relationship," 32.

91. Sartiliot, *Herbarium Verbarium*, 68.

92. Varela et al., *Embodied Mind*, 308; Chemer, *Radical Embodied Cognitive*

we could see the entire universe in a flower, which cannot "be" by itself alone. It can only inter-be as we are all interdependent.[93]

Flowers have a strong visual component that activates the visual and other areas of the brain, creating a stimulating, perceptual experience.[94] There is an endless range of flower colors from pure white to nearly black. Light uses color to adorn the earth with beauty transfiguring everything it touches[95] and is God's spirit in all living things.[96] Light is essential for the plant to blossom. Generally, a plant's natural inclination is to grow toward light.[97] Light can be glimpsed everywhere, in every creature, every life-form, every human being.[98] Light changes with the seasons: in autumn, the sun's sloping rays can look startlingly cinematic, highlighting flowers and plants that are already changing color.[99] Light is deep within and God's spirit is in all living things.[100]

Color is a major determinant when people are selecting flowers.[101] The presence and experience of color are at the very heart of human life[102] and each color evokes its world of feeling and association.[103] Encountering a meadow in summer full of tall, shimmering, yellow buttercups is a wonderful sight.[104] It's hard not to be moved by their serene beauty and the feat of engineering that is in the simple buttercup.[105] Zhang et al. found flowers in white, blue, and, to a lesser extent, purple can play an effective role in relaxation;

Science, 42; Shapiro, *Handbook of Embodied Cognition*.

93. Nhat Hanh, *You Are Here*, 24.

94. Varela et al., *Embodied Mind*, 308.

95. O'Donoghue, *Divine Beauty*, 92.

96. Newell, *Sacred Earth*, 36.

97. Wilson, *Garden for the Senses*, 32.

98. Wilson, *Garden for the Senses*, 32.

99. Wilson, *Garden for the Senses*, 114.

100. Wilson, *Garden for the Senses*, 114.

101. Hansen and Alvarez, "Color in the Landscape."

102. O'Donoghue, *Divine Beauty*, 94.

103. O'Donoghue, *Divine Beauty*, 100.

104. Murray, *Wild Embrace*, 81.

105. Murray, *Wild Embrace*, 81.

flowers in white and warm colors such as orange, yellow, and red can evoke uplifted emotions and deliver better positive affects.[106]

Of all our senses, smell is the memory trigger.[107] The smell of flowers has an intriguing ability to evoke emotions, memories, and visions and has played an important role in the world's spiritual traditions since the dawn of time.[108] Scent can bring back childhood memories as, up until adolescence, smell is a person's most developed sense, having already begun to form in the womb.[109] When a flower smells, it is the result of the olfactory sensory neurons being stimulated by the tiny odor molecules which then travel to the brain where an emotional response and the making and storing of memories are processed.[110] While our sense of smell diminishes with age, our olfactory response can be strengthened by consciously sniffing and identifying the varying components of what we are smelling.[111]

Flower scent is pleasing to humans as the enlightenment of plants brings a fragrance from the realm of spirit.[112] Although we are not all equally receptive to scent, it can stop us in our tracks, take us back to precious times and places in our lives, or create new memories in a way that no other sense can match.[113] Scent is volatile and subject to weather and light levels, as well as to a person's olfactory receptors.[114] Through breathing in the floral perfume, we celebrate our part in the natural miracle of life[115] as it is a connection with the Divine.[116]

106. Zhang et al., "Flowers—Sunshine for the Soul!"

107. Wilson, *Garden for the Senses*, 85.

108. Worwood, *Fragrant Mind*.

109. Wilson, *Garden for the Senses*, 92.

110. Wilson, *Garden for the Senses*, 92.

111. Wilson, *Garden for the Senses*, 92.

112. Tolle, *New Earth*, 3.

113. Wilson, *Garden for the Senses*, 85.

114. Wilson, *Garden for the Senses*, 82.

115. Thompson, "Gardening as Spiritual Practice."

116. Worwood, *Fragrant Mind*, 5.

Worwood draws on the pioneering research of scientists and the insights of leading spiritual teachers in her study of the use of plant fragrance in spirituality. She details how fragrances from essential oils are used in many spiritual practices in Shinto, Buddhist, and Native American rites for healing, prayer, and meditation calling upon the Divine power of fragrance to enrich their spiritual journeys.[117]

Scientists have five key groups for taste: sweet, salty, savory, sour, and bitter.[118] The term "edible" does not always imply that something is pleasant to eat and putting a flower head of borage, whose petals are a memorable blue color, on a dish proves that. The sepals are hairy and the stems and leaves are bristly but its taste is pleasant.[119]

Edward Bach (1886–1936) made a pioneering discovery in medicine when he realized that many symptoms of illness were from emotional states—for example, fear and anger. Through tasting the blossoms of wildflowers and flowers of shrubs and trees, he developed the Bach Flower Remedies, which are commonly used today for emotional and spiritual healing.[120]

When we touch something or something touches us, we feel it through the receptors in the top layers of our skin.[121] Every time a plant is touched, there is an intense physiological response that is part of its distress system which expends energy and diverts it away from the plant's growth.[122] Plants also have a mechanism for halting the distress response.[123] Touching flowering plants can evoke various reactions and emotions. All parts of the hellebore

117. Worwood, *Fragrant Mind*, 10–62.
118. Wilson, *Garden for the Senses*, 62.
119. Wilson, *Garden for the Senses*, 44.
120. Kramer, *New Bach Flower Therapies*.
121. Wilson, *Garden for the Senses*, 32.
122. Wilson, *Garden for the Senses*, 32.
123. Wilson, *Garden for the Senses*, 32.

are toxic.[124] The thorn on the rose feels sharp and the primrose petals feel soft, but to touch aconite is toxic.[125]

Each plant speaks to us through color and sound vibrations that are specific to each energy center within ourselves and defined by the type of soil and climate it lives in.[126] Plants release sound emissions from different organs and at different growth stages or in response to different situations.[127] Khait et al. found that stressed plants emit airborne sounds that can be recorded from a distance.[128] Plants' reactions to noise are based on vibrations.[129] Scientists are investigating the possibility of harnessing good vibrations for increased plant health, which in turn is beneficial for us humans.[130]

When you merge with the energy of the plant, taking on how it feels, grows, touches, and communicates, you hear the voice and the songs of the plant.[131] When the flower is at its peak, surrender and prepare yourself for the sacred medicine of the flower and live as One with all creation.[132]

4. Contemplative Flower Appreciation

The contemplative life belongs to nature, the seasons and cycles of the garden.[133] Seasons encourage us to embrace the paradoxes of struggle and joy, loss and gain, darkness and light, and finding all of it provides growth opportunities.[134] Contemplation is the awakening of the spirit that restores us to our true place in the

124. Dobbs, *Secret Language of Flowers*, 163.

125. Chan, "Aconite Poisoning," 279–85.

126. Pallasdowney, *Voices of Flowers*, 2.

127. Jung et al., "Beyond Chemical Triggers."

128. Khait et al., "Sounds Emitted by Plants."

129. Wilson, *Garden for the Senses*, 152.

130. Wilson, *Garden for the Senses*, 152.

131. Pallasdowney, *Voices of Flowers*, 7.

132. Pallasdowney, *Voices of Flowers*, 7.

133. Versluis, *Awakening the Contemplative Spirit*, 133.

134. Palmer, *Let Your Life Speak*, 96.

cosmos as it reveals our true Divine nature, ending in transfiguration, which is spiritual awakening realizing truth and wisdom for
ourselves and of our world.[135]

Beauty, and our role in co-creating it, lie at the heart of our
spiritual journey.[136] We all share beauty; whether it is a simple
flower or a snowfall, there is no end to beauty for the person
who is aware.[137] Seeing beauty in a flower can awaken humans
to the beauty that is an essential part of their innermost being,
their true nature.[138] The feelings of joy and love are connected to
the first recognition of beauty, the most significant event in the
evolution of human consciousness.[139] Flowers would become for
us an expression in the form of that which is most sacred and
ultimately formless within ourselves, becoming like messengers
from another realm, like a bridge between the world of physical
forms and the formless.[140]

Water is essential for flowers to grow with varying amounts
required depending on the stages of growth. In Celtic wisdom, water connects us to the womb from which all things have come.[141]
In ancient Egypt, every temple had a sacred lake symbolizing the
original waters of creation.[142] Water is part of our genesis and essential to our well-being.[143] All water is sacred, and for the sake of
the earth, the sacredness of water must be protected.[144] Destroying
or blocking water sources such as wells is symbolic of the inner
well of the soul being denied individually and collectively.[145] When
we know that the inner well of our being is sacred, we will serve at

---

135. Versluis, *Awakening the Contemplative Spirit*, 140.

136. Fox, *Creation Spirituality*, 21.

137. Fox, *Creation Spirituality*, 49.

138. Tolle, *New Earth*, 3.

139. Tolle, *New Earth*, 2.

140. Tolle, *New Earth*, 2–3.

141. Newell, *Sacred Earth*, 65–66.

142. Naydler, *Gardening as a Sacred Art*, 16.

143. Newell, *Sacred Earth*, 66.

144. Newell, *Sacred Earth*, 66.

145. Newell, *Sacred Earth*, 66.

that well, we will midwife the new beginnings waiting to be born deep within us and we can serve at these birthings.[146]

St. Brigid helps us to remember that the earth and the human soul are sacred.[147] Produced over eons by the earth's natural processes, the soil is the basis of all life as it's the growing medium for plants that support the world's ecosystems and sustain living creatures at all levels in the food chain, including us humans, thus deserving our nurturing and care.[148] Everything comes from the soil and returns to the soil and through the soil, we are all held, related, and interconnected.[149] The soil is a metaphor for the entire natural system.[150] If we take care of the soil, the soil will take care of us.[151] All living things depend on the soil and soil treats all living beings equally, unconditionally and indiscriminately.[152] Soil microbes *Mycobacterium vaccae* help plants sequester carbon from the atmosphere and have a visceral effect on humans by activating our brains to release more serotonin, impacting our mood and cognitive function and boosting our immune system.[153]

The Divine is to be met in the depths of darkness as well as in the light. Daring the dark means entering nothingness and letting it be nothingness while it works its mystery on us.[154] A return to the dark is also a return to our origins, we were conceived in the dark, lived our life in the womb in the dark and were from all eternity in the dark heart of the God that preceded the creation of fire and light.[155] Spiritual path two, *via negativa*, is about being at home in the dark, our letting go and letting it be.[156] We can choose

146. Newell, *Sacred Earth*, 66.

147. Newell, *Sacred Earth*, 68.

148. Ferguson, *Old Wives Lore for Gardeners*, 27.

149. Kumar, *Soil, Soul, Society*, 17.

150. Kumar, *Soil, Soul, Society*, 17.

151. Kumar, *Soil, Soul, Society*, 17.

152. Kumar, *Soil, Soul, Society*, 17.

153. Wilson, *Garden for the Senses*, 31.

154. Fox, *Creation Spirituality*, 20.

155. Fox, *Creation Spirituality*, 20.

156. Fox, *Creation Spirituality*, 20.

to stand on a ground that is not riddled with fault lines of fear, a ground that will support us, from which we can lead others toward a more trustworthy, more hopeful, more faithful way of being in the world.[157]

Time and soil provide fertile soil for the germination of ideas, as opening our senses to our surroundings can be surprisingly rewarding.[158] It took Versluis years to understand what kind of ground it was, what it liked and didn't like, what grew well and what grew poorly, what weeds became pests and how to overcome them.[159] If your soil is heavy clay loam, Versluis claims it needs no irrigation even in the worst of droughts.[160] The soil warms up slowly in the spring and you cannot sow your seed too early or you will have a poor crop. In the contemplative life, while we long for some sudden transformation, we need to remember what kind of soil we are working with and where we already are.[161]

In every seed is the promise of thousands of forests.[162] The seed must not be hoarded, it must give its intelligence to the fertile ground.[163] All the flowers of tomorrow are in the seeds of today.[164] Through its giving, its unseen energy flows into material manifestation.[165] Taking the tiniest seed and placing it in the best possible soil, caring for it as it grows, and marveling at the changes that come over it gives us great reward while standing as a poetic symbol of transformation.[166] If I want to create happiness, I must live out the expression "what you sow is what you reap," I must consciously sow the seeds of happiness.[167]

157. Palmer, *Let Your Life Speak*, 94.

158. Murray, *Wild Embrace*, 76.

159. Versluis, *Awakening the Contemplative Spirit*, 84.

160. Versluis, *Awakening the Contemplative Spirit*, 84.

161. Versluis, *Awakening the Contemplative Spirit*, 84.

162. Chopra, *Seven Spiritual Laws*, 29.

163. Chopra, *Seven Spiritual Laws*, 29.

164. Ferguson, *Old Wives Lore for Gardeners*, 45.

165. Chopra, *Seven Spiritual Laws*, 29.

166. Vinje, "Spirit of Gardening."

167. Chopra, *Seven Spiritual Laws*, 39.

Our soul is a bundle of consciousness that has seeds of karma, memory, and desire. By becoming conscious of these seeds of manifestation, you become a conscious generator of reality.[168] The seeds we sow in the garden must die buried in the earth before they can be reborn into the new green and growing life of the plant.[169] The "seed" of the true self is what is planted in the world at our birth to the "journey" we take through the darkness toward the light.[170] Seeds move through their life stages in an endless cycle of seasons and the cycle of seasons reminds us that our journey never ends.[171] Our lives participate in the myth of eternal return, we circle around and spiral down, Who am I and Whose am I?[172] In the Christian tradition, Good Friday and Easter mark the culmination of this outward death and inward life.[173] This is the most profound mystery that is inherent in the very seeds that we sow.[174]

Flowers such as dandelions, daffodils, and primroses offer signs of hope through their new life in spring. Summer fills with abundance while autumn is a season of great beauty and decline as its abundance decays toward winter's death.[175] Nature scatters the seeds that will bring new growth in the spring and scatters them with amazing abandon. My delight in the autumn colors is tinged with melancholy, a sense of impending loss that is only heightened by the beauty all around it.[176] While flowers die, many of them resurrect again. Dying is part of life. O'Donoghue says while death is a huge mystery, it brings out the fire and fiber at the heart of beauty.[177]

Winter is the season of serenity, that time when our roots grow deeper into the rich loam of spiritual life. This is what is

168. Chopra, *Seven Spiritual Laws*, 48.

169. Versluis, *Awakening the Contemplative Spirit*, 134.

170. Palmer, *Let Your Life Speak*, 95.

171. Palmer, *Let Your Life Speak*, 95.

172. Palmer, *Let Your Life Speak*, 95.

173. Versluis, *Awakening the Contemplative Spirit*, 134.

174. Versluis, *Awakening the Contemplative Spirit*, 134.

175. Palmer, *Let Your Life Speak*, 98.

176. Palmer, *Let Your Life Speak*, 98.

177. O'Donoghue, *Divine Beauty*, 225.

meant by the "dark night of the soul," that time when the Divine presence itself seems to withdraw.[178] The seeds have died buried in the earth before they are reborn into the new plant.[179] Winter is the time of contemplative life, for when outward life seems desiccated, brown, and dead, all of nature turns inward.[180] During winter, the most important work takes place; when it appears that nothing is happening, all the work is taking place in the darkness of the cold winter.[181] It is then that the soil replenishes itself, hidden from the activity of other seasons. Without this stillness and chill, without the darkness, the other seasons would not have such power and vitality.[182]

The beautiful conditions for rebirth are being created for spring through mud and the decayed vegetable matter (humus) feeding the roots of plants.[183] The words "humid", "human", "humility", and "humus" all come from the same root.[184] The soil is so fertile, yet humble. When humans lose humility, they are no longer humans.[185] This helps Palmer to understand that events that put mud on his face may be the fertile soil in which something new can happen.[186]

The smallest and most tender shoots insist on having their way in spring, coming up through ground that only a few weeks ago looked like it would never grow anything again.[187] The crocuses and snowdrops don't bloom for long but their appearance is a harbinger of hope.[188] Hope grows at a geometric rate.[189] Spring

178. Versluis, *Awakening the Contemplative Spirit*, 133.

179. Versluis, *Awakening the Contemplative Spirit*, 134.

180. Versluis, *Awakening the Contemplative Spirit*, 134.

181. Versluis, *Awakening the Contemplative Spirit*, 134.

182. Versluis, *Awakening the Contemplative Spirit*, 134.

183. Palmer, *Let Your Life Speak*, 103.

184. Kumar, *Soil, Soul, Society*, 17.

185. Palmer, *Let Your Life Speak*, 103.

186. Palmer, *Let Your Life Speak*, 103.

187. Palmer, *Let Your Life Speak*, 104.

188. Palmer, *Let Your Life Speak*, 104.

189. Palmer, *Let Your Life Speak*, 104.

teaches Palmer to look for the green stems of possibilities, for the intuitive hunch that may turn into a larger insight, for the glance or touch that may thaw a frozen relationship, for the stranger's act of kindness that makes the world seem hospitable again.[190] Late spring is potlatch time in the natural world, a great giveaway of blooming beyond all necessity and reason, it would appear, for no reason other than the sheer joy of it all.[191]

When you are alert and contemplate a flower, there is an inner opening, however slight, into the realm of spirit, which is why the lotus flower is the central symbol of Buddhism.[192] Each plant is a contemplative gift from the earth.[193] Just as the earth is forever pushing forth new life, so it is with the human soul.[194] The contemplative flower gardener or observer says spiritual awakening is a process as one's practices are rooted in attention, stillness, silence, presence, awareness, solitude, as well as struggle, relinquishment, and surrender to facilitate the person to unitive awareness and to mediate it.[195]

Newell states that we need to fall in love with flowers and all things to do with them.[196] Tolle believes that we are here to enable the Divine purpose of the universe to unfold. That is how important we are.[197] Watch any flower and it will teach you acceptance of what is, let it teach you *being*, let it teach you integrity which means to be one with yourself, to be real, let it teach you how to live and how to die and how not to make living and dying into a problem.[198] We are in the midst of a great reawakening of the sacredness of the earth and the human soul with an explosion of earth awareness in

---

190. Palmer, *Let Your Life Speak*, 104.

191. Palmer, *Let Your Life Speak*, 104.

192. Tolle, *New Earth*, 5.

193. Versluis, *Awakening the Contemplative Spirit*, 81.

194. Newell, *Sacred Earth*, 65.

195. Christie, *Insurmountable Darkness of Love*, 10.

196. Newell, *Sacred Earth*, 253.

197. Tolle, *Power of Now*, Introduction.

198. Tolle, *Power of Now*, 157.

our human consciousness.[199] This is *the via positiva*, being in awe, wonder, and mystery of nature and all things, each of whom is a word of God.[200]

5. Conclusion

Humanity and flowering plants have evolved over the millennia. Flowers, through their sensory arousal, awaken us humans to the beauty that is an essential part of our innermost being, our true nature. The color, smell, taste, and touch in particular of the flower capture our attention in so many ways. Flowers are an expression in the form of that which is most sacred within ourselves being like a bridge between heaven and earth and connecting us within and to the outside world.

This perspective of the relationship between humans and flowers is limited in the literature[201] with minimal disaggregation by age, gender, religion, or culture. When studies have taken place, they tended to be with small numbers of people often using images or artificial flowers. There is a great deal of literature about gardening and spiritual claims by florists on their business websites which are usually without academic backup.

In my next chapter, I will discuss understanding spirituality.

199. Tolle, *Power of Now*, 157.
200. Fox, *Creation Spirituality*, 20.
201. Huss et al., "Humans' Relationship to Flowers," 32.

Chapter Two

Understanding Spirituality

1. Introduction

I WILL DESCRIBE MY spirituality framework based on my lived spiritual experience. I have chosen the Praxis of Authenticity as my spiritual framework as it is based on a lived experience of my subjective state recognizing the dynamic orientation toward beauty, intelligibility, truth, goodness, and love through attending, interpreting, judging, and deciding on my knowing. I also chose Creation Spirituality to deepen and complement my spiritual framework. I will define my understanding of spirituality and will discuss spirituality as shared by others that resonate with me for my thesis topic.

2. Definition of Spirituality

As we are one with our soul sickness and with our body sickness, we can be one with our healing and liberation.[1] We are constantly searching for God in our hearts.[2] To be spiritual is to be fully alive, breathing deeply, as we journey on a life-filled path to the inner

---

1. Fox, *Creation Spirituality*, xiii.
2. Griffiths, *Cosmic Revelation*, 45.

person in a spirit-filled way of living.[3] Spirituality understood with reference to what is fundamental for living, namely breathing, is, like our breathing, a moving rather than static reality. The breathing process involves the recurring and rhythmic movement of breathing in and breathing out.[4] As one does that, they experience and attend to their living spirit present and active in their embodied self, which moves them to transform and integrate.[5]

Schneiders writes of spirituality as the experience of conscious involvement in the project of life-integration through self-transcendence toward the horizon of ultimate value one perceives.[6] Spirituality is our primordial source for our search for meaning while also offering us a much more coherent route to a comprehensive experience of Divine revelation.[7] Spirituality is the way in which our values and beliefs are apparent in our words and our actions. Our spirituality is evident in the way we spend our time and how we invest our energies, honor relationships, and treat our planet.[8] My spirituality engages with my core values of justice, love, peace, and freedom "with the foundational value-orientation which belongs to the mutual existence of person and planet alike."[9]

Spirituality can be considered an inherent or constitutive dimension of a person. This dimension refers to a foundational and permeating sensibility in the human, which is the root of the transformation and integration toward what is beautiful, intelligible, true, good, and loving that takes place in the lives of individuals, groups, societies, and traditions.[10] It exists at a root and core level in the sense that it makes such transformation and integration, and their quality, possible.[11]

3. Fox, *Creation Spirituality*, 11–12.

4. O'Sullivan, "Authenticity as a Spirituality Process."

5. O'Sullivan, "Authenticity as a Spirituality Process."

6. Schneiders, "Approaches," 16.

7. Ó Murchú, *Reclaiming Spirituality*, 78.

8. NicUaithuas, "Spirituality, Social Concern, and Gender."

9. Ó Murchú, *Reclaiming Spirituality*, 172.

10. O'Sullivan, "Authenticity as a Spirituality Process."

11. O'Sullivan, "Authenticity as a Spirituality Process."

This fits with Frohlich's description of spirituality, which she says studies the living and concrete human person in dynamic transformation toward the fullness of life.[12] Spirituality is now generally thought to be native to anyone, whether they are religious or not. Spirituality concerns what is holistic, involves a quest for meaning, is linked to "thriving," and asks for a self-reflective existence as opposed to an unexamined life. Within this definition, there are several religious spiritualties such as Jewish, Christian, Islamic, Hindu, and Buddhist.[13]

3. Spiritual Frameworks

3.1. Lived Spirituality as a Praxis of Authenticity

O'Sullivan's Praxis of Authenticity recognizes that all lives are spiritual at an anthropological level, so the language and the framework can include everyone while recognizing that people will differ in their spirituality depending on the horizon of ultimate value and meaning that guides their common, radical, and dynamic self-transcending orientation. It is open to studying all aspects of life because the dynamic desire of knowing and choosing is unlimited.[14]

Authenticity refers to how I perform in consciousness regarding how to know and choose objectively. It is a lived experience of existing in our subjectivity in a state of dynamic orientation toward beauty, intelligibility, truth, goodness, and love, and with inherent norms of how to attend, interpret, judge, and decide in our knowing and choosing for the sake of fidelity to that orientation. This framework for studying lived experience in terms of spirituality guides us, foundationally and methodologically, toward contextualized beauty, truth, goodness, and love.[15] By "consciousness" O'Sullivan means the self-presence that is the condition of the

12. Frohlich, "Critical Interiority," 77.

13. Sheldrake, *Spirituality*, 8.

14. O'Sullivan, "Authenticity as a Spirituality Process."

15. O'Sullivan, "Spiritual Capital and Authentic Subjectivity," 7.

possibility to even be unconscious! It is precisely because of this self-presence that the unconscious can be brought to awareness and become present to us.[16]

We desire to be and to do good because that is how we are, ultimately—"God saw what God had made was good" and this is verified by the Praxis of Authenticity in knowing and choosing.[17] The Divine meaning of creation is not derived from us humans; it is the source and well-being and we humans are the derivative species! Reconnecting with that inner, vital, bestowed energy drives us toward a sense of purpose and meaning in our lives. Something deep within us compels us to seek meaning which is primal, subconscious, and fundamental to the very existence of human existence, just as it is central to the unfolding of cosmic evolution itself. Seeking meaning is the overriding governing force behind everything in *being*.[18] *Being* is what is accessible deep within yourself, it's your true nature, which you can only know when your mind is still and you are present in the Now.[19] The present moment holds the key to liberation.[20]

3.2. Creation Spirituality

Creation is all things and us and is us in relationship with all things, all beings, the ones we see and the invisible ones, flowers, rocks, animals, trees, galaxies, and plants.[21] Creation is all space, all time, all things past, present, and future with relation at its core.[22] Creation is always making new, enticing us to be fully present to all space and all time.[23] The whole of humanity is here in each of us depending on our capacity to go out in love to others and to

16. O'Sullivan, "Authenticity as a Spirituality Process."
17. O'Sullivan, "Reflexive and Transformative Subjectivity," 173–82.
18. Ó Murchú, *Reclaiming Spirituality*, 60.
19. Tolle, *Power of Now*, 10.
20. Tolle, *Power of Now*, 19.
21. Fox, *Creation Spirituality*, 7–8.
22. Fox, *Creation Spirituality*, 8–9.
23. Fox, *Creation Spirituality*, 10.

be embraced in love by others, a task which we are all moving toward.[24]

Cosmic revelation is in the heart of humans. Hindus believe that God is dancing in the heart of creation and in the heart of every human.[25] The Hindu sees the whole world as being continually created and destroyed, all is coming into being and dying, and birth and death go on all the time, which is the rhythm of creation sustained by God. As we accept the coming into being, we also accept the passing out of being—the creation and the destruction.[26] Things are not lost or destroyed, they are transfigured.[27] Cosmic revelation is based on the belief that God is revealed in creation and in the human soul.[28] All the beauty of creation is present here for our joy and for our thanksgiving.[29] The Hindu tradition holds the sun and the moon, the flowers and trees with reverence, as God is in the midst of them.[30]

Everything in Hinduism is sacred as God is immanent and is in everything: the earth, water, air, plants, animals, and all people.[31] In Judaism, the tradition holds that God is infinitely above the heavens and comes down to earth,[32] while the Christian view is that humans are called to be in harmony with nature and with God, which we now realize that we have lost.[33]

Each person has a unique destiny. Once this sense of destiny is awakened, one comes into rhythm with one's life. Rhythm is the secret key to balance and belonging. To be spiritual is to be in rhythm.[34] The rhythm of the seasons outside in nature is also

24. Griffiths, *Cosmic Revelation*, 131.
25. Griffiths, *Cosmic Revelation*, 41.
26. Griffiths, *Cosmic Revelation*, 42.
27. Griffiths, *Cosmic Revelation*, 127.
28. Griffiths, *Cosmic Revelation*, 109.
29. Griffiths, *Cosmic Revelation*, 131.
30. Griffiths, *Cosmic Revelation*, 22.
31. Griffiths, *Cosmic Revelation*, 23.
32. Griffiths, *Cosmic Revelation*, 23.
33. Griffiths, *Cosmic Revelation*, 27.
34. Griffiths, *Cosmic Revelation*, 114.

active in our hearts.[35] When the first innocent, infant-like flower appears on the earth, one senses nature stirring beneath the surface. The wonderful colors and the new life that the earth receives bring much joy and hope.[36]

4. Conclusion

My spirituality is centered on understanding that "creation is all things and us and is us in relationship with all things, all beings, the ones we see and the invisible ones, flowers, rocks, animals, trees, galaxies, and plants."[37] Creation is always making new, enticing us to be fully present to all space and all time.[38]

My spiritual journey begins with awe, wonder, and falling in love, be it with a species of wildflower of which "there are at least 10,000 species on this planet"[39] or other flowers. The awe I feel is stirring within me, my realization of my interconnectedness with flowers and with other creatures and people on this planet. As I explore the spirituality of flowers, my call is to be still, compassionate, and joyful as I awaken to the flourishing of the gift of flowers to humanity.

In the next chapter, I will describe my rationale for how I explored flower appreciation and the methods I used for my research.

35. Griffiths, *Cosmic Revelation*, 204–5.

36. Griffiths, *Cosmic Revelation*, 205–6.

37. Fox, *Creation Spirituality*, 7–8.

38. Fox, *Creation Spirituality*, 10.

39. Fox, *Creation Spirituality*, 19.

Chapter Three

Exploring Flower Appreciation

1. Introduction

IN THIS CHAPTER I will describe my research methods, Form-Descriptive Method and Reading for Transformation, that helped me explore and answer my research question: Is flower appreciation a participation in a Divine-human transformation process and, if so, how is it being expressed?

2. Rationale for Selected Research Approaches

Spirituality is our primordial source for our search for meaning while also offering us a much more coherent route to a comprehensive experience of Divine revelation.[1] Frohlich believes "every research project is an activity of the searching human spirit."[2] In my searching spirit, I have chosen to use the first person (my own observations of change through journaling) and second person (reviewing lived spiritual experiences of selected authors of books) to research the Divine-human transformation of flower appreciation. My choice is based on the very limited literature available on the

1. Ó Murchú, *Reclaiming Spirituality*, 78.
2. Frohlich, "Spirit, Spirituality, and Contemplative Method," 133–34.

Divine-human transformation. For the purposes of this research, I have chosen to review the limited literature that I have found to assess and evaluate what and how it describes the Divine-human transformation through flower appreciation.

Varela says the researcher must be "an empathic resonator with experiences that are familiar to her and which find in her a resonant chord," which does not put me inside another's experience but at least gets me into the same room.[3] As a spirituality researcher, I will only be able to grasp something of the experiential process of transformation that is being depicted in my selected books based on engagement in my experiential spiritual process of transformation. This means that my questions and reflection about what is being described derive from a basis of my lived experience rather than simply from theoretical analysis.[4]

O'Sullivan says the researcher detects the spirited desire in humans for authenticity at the level of her experience and capacity. This is done through experiencing a call or push in my interiority to become aware of and attend to all the relevant data regarding the text[5] that I will read and through my journaling and reflection. This dynamism of authenticity will be detected through my questioning of the data and taking into account my subjectivity in terms of the quality with which I make judgments of the value of what I ought to do based on that knowledge. This means that my research is a "self-implicating activity and implicating for those who engage with the research."[6] Doing research according to this methodology of authentic subjectivity is a contemplative, rigorous, and open-ended spiritual practice allowing the researcher onto the path to beauty, truth, goodness, and love as ultimate dimensions of reality.[7]

---

3. Varela and Shear, "First-Person Methodologies," 10.

4. Frohlich, "Spirit, Spirituality, and Contemplative Method," 133–34.

5. O'Sullivan, "Authentic Subjectivity," 271–77.

6. O'Sullivan, "Authentic Subjectivity," 271–77.

7. O'Sullivan, "Authentic Subjectivity," 271–77.

3. Research Approaches

3.1. Form-Descriptive Approach

In researching the Divine-human transformational process of flower appreciation, I will use the three-fold structure of the Form-Descriptive Method (phenomenological) developed by Waaijman.[8]

3.1.1. Demarcate the Form

The form of the phenomenon of flower appreciation goes back to pre-10,000 BC when our ancestors lived in a transcendent[9] mode in an equalitarian and cooperative rapport with the earth.[10] They acknowledged the nearness of the Divine power, recognizing the interdependence of everything in the universe that needs everything else.[11]

In the ancient world, natural phenomena were normal subjects with inner qualities and emotions just like us human beings, nature having a rich inner life, with the soul of the human being shared in the soul-life of nature.[12] The earth was understood to be a living organism, the embodiment of the Great Mother Goddess, who nurtured and sustained life with prodigious fertility and overflowing abundance. It would have been inconceivable that we rupture the womb that nourishes us.[13] Through the agricultural revolution until about 3,000 BC, humanity developed a deeper sense that earth, as a great nourishing Mother, was a supreme

8. Waaijman, *Forms, Foundations, Methods*, 601–88.

9. Transcendence denotes the openness and willingness to rise above our daily and mundane concerns in the acknowledgment that a life force (what Christians refer to as God) higher than us influences and governs the course of events. Transcendence is the invitation to live and work with that life force, which adds depth and meaning to our daily interactions within the word itself. Ó Murchú, *Reclaiming Spirituality*, 64.

10. Ó Murchú, *Reclaiming Spirituality*, 63.

11. Ó Murchú, *Reclaiming Spirituality*, 93.

12. Naydler, *Gardening as a Sacred Art*, 20–21.

13. Ó Murchú, *Reclaiming Spirituality*, 70.

friend, always to be treated with gentleness, care, dignity, and profound respect for its inherent laws and values.[14]

3.1.2. *External Horizon*

For us humans to attain the fullness of life, we need plants, fish, and the many biochemical processes that fertilize creation with beauty and nourishment; destroy any one aspect and human survival becomes precarious—in fact, threatened with extinction.[15]

The secularization of sacred spaces such as gardens began during the first century BC when the Romans conceived of gardens[16] as essentially a creation by humans for humans.[17] The sense that the world of spirit was retreating, accompanied by the growing feeling of detachment from nature, was increasingly seen as something "out there."[18] Since then, patriarchy, androcentrism,[19] and sexism have prevailed, undermining a more meaningful relationship with our planet Earth and with all life forms within it.[20] We sought to dominate the Divine power by taking to ourselves the perceived role of God as the all-knowing being.[21] This led to our current social and cultural dislocation, losing touch with the spirit within, the fundamental nature of life, our own and that of the universe.[22] We need to reconnect with the cosmic and planetary womb that begets, sustains, and nourishes us and articulate the interrelatedness inherent to both humanity and creation at large.[23]

---

14. Ó Murchú, *Reclaiming Spirituality*, 72.

15. Ó Murchú, *Reclaiming Spirituality*, 18.

16. Robinson, *English Flower Garden*, 86.

17. Naydler, *Gardening as a Sacred Art*, 32.

18. Naydler, *Gardening as a Sacred Art*, 26.

19. Anthropocentrism refers to our focus on the human and the belief that we are the final purpose of the cosmos. Guthrie, *Faces in the Church*, 6.

20. Ó Murchú, *Reclaiming Spirituality*, 102.

21. Ó Murchú, *Reclaiming Spirituality*, 72.

22. Ó Murchú, *Reclaiming Spirituality*, 59.

23. Ó Murchú, *Reclaiming Spirituality*, 58–59.

3.1.3. *Internal Horizon of the Form*

My key research question is, Is flower appreciation a participation in a Divine-human transformation process and, if so, how is it being expressed?

As we become disengaged from our primal and spiritual roots, we behave in frightened ways, the head and the heart move in opposite directions, detrimental to both and to everything else we engage with in our daily lives.[24] We can understand the human only through the earth and until the human is understood as a dimension of the earth, we have no secure basis for understanding any aspect of being human.[25] It is imminently important for humanity and for earth that we reconnect with that sacred epic of the evolution of creation.[26]

In researching the phenomenological, which is the spirituality observed in everyday phenomena[27] such as people's engagement with flowers, I will assess what Divine-human transformation process is being disclosed within the given form with regard to God-relatedness and world-relatedness.[28] My aim in this level of description is to unpack it from within the books that I read and through my journaling.

Lonergan says the human spirit instinctively follows the path of expansion of consciousness. He used the term "interiority analysis" to describe one's ability to identify and appropriate the operations involved in the dynamic unfolding of one's cognitive process through experiences, seeking understanding, and critically evaluating that understanding in order to verify it, and finally to ask, What should I do about this?[29] I will apply Lonergan's list of operations: "seeing, hearing, touching, smelling, tasting, inquiring, imagining, understanding, conceiving, formulating,

---

24. Ó Murchú, *Reclaiming Spirituality*, 59.

25. Berry, *Dream of the Earth*, 219.

26. Ó Murchú, *Reclaiming Spirituality*, 51.

27. Waaijman, *Forms, Foundations, Methods*, 601–88.

28. Waaijman, *Forms, Foundations, Methods*, 601–88.

29. Lonergan, *Phenomenology and Logic*, 314–17.

reflecting, and weighing the evidence, judging, deliberating, evaluating, deciding, speaking, writing"[30] as I carry out my research. I will choose interpretative categories to understand the form, such as solitude, and creativity to assess how the authors and I reconnect with that inner, vital, bestowed energy and how it drives us toward a sense of purpose and meaning in our lives.

3.2. Transformation of the Researcher Approach

This proposes the Transformation of the Researcher as a research method as I study the selected books listed below and reflect on my journaling. Schneiders claims reading for transformation goes beyond simply discovering what the text says is true, and, if so, in what sense and what the personal consequences for the reader and others might be.[31]

The essential dynamic for transpersonal and spiritual research is the researchers' willingness to engage in research as a journey of transformation that fully implicates their understanding of the topic.[32] Transformative learning happens when individuals have an urge toward self-actualization.[33] Maslow's concept of self-actualization includes acceptance of self and others and having peak experiences that lead to personal transformation.[34] Transformative learning is described as cognitive and rational, imaginative and intuitive, spiritual, related to individuation, relational, and relating to social change, to name just a few of the most common perspectives.[35]

As I apply the Transformation of the Researcher method of research, I will investigate the conditions of "the possibility of a spiritually transformative encounter"[36] with the selected books

30. Lonergan, *Method in Theology*, 6.

31. Schneiders, *Revelatory Text*, 14.

32. Anderson, "Transformative Research Methods," 95–103.

33. Taylor et al., *Handbook of Transformative Learning*, 14.

34. Whitmore, *Coaching for Performance*, 17.

35. Taylor et al., *Handbook of Transformative Learning*, 17.

36. McAloon, "Reading for Transformation," 184.

during my research. I anticipate many accounts of spiritual experiences through my journaling and book reviews will strongly affirm a sense of being taken beyond myself into oneness with Divine love. In approaching my research, I begin with recognizing and claiming my spiritual investment in the authenticity and fruits of my research as I seek "to sound the contemplative depths to bring forth fruits of transforming insight for a larger human community."[37]

4. Ethical Approval

I sought and received ethical approval from the South East Technical University (SETU) Board on February 10, 2023. As I will not be interviewing anyone for my research, the risk of violating ethical requirements is minimal.

5. Data Collection Method

5.1. Journaling

I observed, reflected, and explored the following in my journaling:

- my experience of walking in nature;
- observing the influence of flowers, be it within my home garden, in public spaces, in bouquets of flowers that I received, or anywhere that I noticed flowers; and
- my reflection on these experiences which formed an aspect of my data collection.

5.2. Review of Selected Books

I selected books based on my preliminary review of the lived experiences of the authors regarding their experience of flower appreciation. Frohlich identifies spirituality as an academic discipline

---

37. Frohlich, "Contemplative Method," 15.

because its central object of study is the experience of being an embodied human spirit in the dynamic movement toward the fullness of life. This approach makes it possible to study the spiritual experiences of all people regardless of their backgrounds.[38] The essential qualities proposed place attributes such as intuition and immediate apprehension as central to my approach as I will intuitively "lean into" experiences that are already present.[39]

The contemporary authors and books that I have chosen are:

1. *The Twelve Gifts from the Garden: Life Lessons for Peace and Well-Being* by Charlene Costanzo.[40] Costanzo writes about her learning, empowerment, and enrichment as she journeyed with flowers, plants, and nature on Sanibel Island off the coast of Florida.

2. *Dear Friend and Gardener: Letters on Life and Gardening* by Beth Chatto and Christopher Lloyd.[41] The authors interweave their thoughts and emotions of their flower gardening with other aspects of their lives through their letters to each other. Chatto's experience of gardening began in Elmstead Market, Essex while Lloyd's garden is where he grew up in Great Dixter in East Sussex.

3. *Zen Flowers: Contemplation through Creativity* by Harumi Nishi.[42] Nishi provides an inspirational guide to finding true contentment through contemplation and the creation of flower displays inspired by *ikebana*, the traditional Japanese art of flower arranging.

4. *Garden Maker: Growing a Life of Beauty and Wonder with Flowers* by Christie Purifoy.[43] Purifoy reflects the glory and majesty of the Creator and brings a little bit of heaven down to earth as

38. Frohlich, "Spirit, Spirituality, and Contemplative Method," 132.
39. Braud and Anderson, *Transpersonal Research Methods*, 71–76.
40. Costanzo, *Twelve Gifts*.
41. Chatto and Lloyd, *Dear Friend and Gardener*.
42. Nishi, *Zen Flowers*.
43. Christie Purifoy, *Garden Maker*.

she grows her beautiful flowers in her garden in Pennsylvania. She helps to unearth the simple delights of growing garden flowers and invites the reader to discover the innumerable joys and wonders to be found in the flower garden.

6. Conclusion

I will use two methods, Form-Descriptive and Transformation of the Researcher, to research if and how the Divine-human transformation process is expressed through flower appreciation. I will collect my data by reviewing selected contemporary authors and my journaling of the reflections and experiences of flower appreciation.

As I make sense of the purpose and meaning in our lives through flower appreciation, I will use the five senses as well as inquiring, imagining, understanding, conceiving, reflecting, and evaluating as I collect my data. I will be concerned with freedom, autonomy, and choice throughout my transformational learning and authenticity. I will discuss this and the joy, beauty, scent, color, and resilience of flowers in my next chapter.

Chapter Four

Joy, Beauty, Scent, Color, and Resilience of Flowers

1. Introduction

MY RESEARCH QUESTION: Is flower appreciation a participation in a Divine-human transformation process and, if so, how is it being expressed?

2. Qualitative Data Analysis

2.1. Reflective Thematic Analysis

Data was collected by reading four selected books[1] and through my journaling.[2] As a Reflexive Researcher, I am "seeking awareness and new possibilities" through "thoughtful and (self) questioning, identifying and interrogating my values, choices and practices within my research process and the influence of these on knowledge generated."[3] Reflexivity is a journey, not a destination,

---

1. See ch. 3, sec. 5.2 "Review of Selected Books," 35–36.
2. My journal period was from January 6 to May 29, 2023.
3. Berger, "Now I See It, Now I Don't," 219–34.

of an ongoing process of reflection.[4] I constantly questioned what I was reading and journaled what resonated with me as I read the books to ensure I got answers to my research question. My search for a relevant description that resonated with my own experience was personal. It was a yearning to seek external validation and amplification of a rather common yet unspoken experience.[5] My "unique ways of knowing facilitated the organic evolution" of my research process.[6] Applying this approach, information and transformation were inseparable through the integration of thought, feelings, and intuition.[7]

I used Thematic Analysis[8] for identifying, analyzing, and reporting themes that emerged from my data. This approach helped me organize my rich data and to interpret various aspects of my research topic. I was flexible by being inductive, interpreting my journaling findings and what the authors wrote. I was deductive by seeking to see what themes came through. After rereading my data several times, I coded by yellow highlighting significant words and phrases. Coding is a process and practice where one works systematically through a dataset, identifying segments of data that appear potentially interesting, relevant, or meaningful for the research question.[9] Analysis is a process of meaning-making at the intersection of the researcher, the dataset, and analytic and data contexts.[10] Through using "analytic sensibility by reading and interpreting data to produce insights" into my dataset "that go beyond the semantic level,"[11] I noticed connections between existing literature.

---

4. Braun and Clarke, *Thematic Analysis*, 15.

5. Braud and Anderson, *Transpersonal Research Methods*, 72.

6. Anderson and Braud, *Transforming Self and Others*, 15.

7. Anderson and Braud, *Transforming Self and Others*, 15.

8. Anderson and Braud, *Transforming Self and Others*, 79.

9. Braun and Clarke, *Thematic Analysis*, 35.

10. Braun and Clarke, *Thematic Analysis*, 45.

11. Braun and Clarke, *Thematic Analysis*, 44.

I then generated themes by looking at the "cluster of codes, which described broader, shared meanings."[12] Through developing and reviewing my selected themes, I accepted the necessity of relinquishing a substantial amount of valuable data and instead focused on my research question, existing knowledge, and the wider context of my research[13] which led me to refine, define, and name my themes.[14] Please see the appendix for my data analysis. Self-attention disclosed my spirit of authenticity at work methodologically directing it to beauty, intelligibility, truth, goodness, and love.[15] It also means that my research is a self-implicating activity and implicating for those who engage with the research.[16]

Writing my findings was in itself "a form of contemplation, a dwelling with and in the Word."[17] Documenting is an integral part of the analytic process of thematic analysis, and through writing, initially informally and then formally,[18] I have clarity in sharing my findings of the emerging themes.

3. Presentation of Findings: Emerging Themes

The pure essence of mystagogical research is the mystery that is revealed through the data. The books and my journal produced a rich and substantial volume of data. The following five emerging themes are:

12. Braun and Clarke, *Thematic Analysis*, 35.

13. Braun and Clarke, *Thematic Analysis*, 35.

14. Braun and Clarke, *Thematic Analysis*, 36.

15. Lonergan, *Method in Theology*, 9.

16. Lonergan, *Method in Theology*, 9; Anderson, "Transformative Research Methods," 95–103.

17. Versluis, *Awakening the Contemplative Spirit*, 62.

18. Braun and Clarke, *Thematic Analysis*, 36.

- Love and Joy
- Beauty, Scent, and Color
- Resilience
- Gratitude
- Awakening.

3.1. Love and Joy

Nishi says flowers bloom everywhere and in your heart.[19] Purifoy believes flowers are rooted in love, growing them because she is *in love* with flowers, with their enchanting beauty and mysterious scents,[20] which is a way of giving and receiving love.[21] Purifoy feels this love as if the roots of her life are deep in something ancient and powerful, something mysterious and precious.[22] I expressed my awe through journaling, "realizing the soil is billions of years old and standing on it for one minute, grounds me as I feel that ancient earth supporting me."[23]

By putting love into flower arranging, Nishi says you help foster an atmosphere of serenity and peace.[24] Nishi's "Global Flower" arrangement can be a single flower, like the passion flower, to shine like a lone star and illuminate the beauty of the universe,[25] or a beautiful hydrangea bloom set against a pale blue background, suggesting the basic unity of all things within the universe.[26] This triggered me to journal:

19. Nishi, *Zen Flowers*, 58.
20. Purifoy, *Garden Maker*, 8.
21. Purifoy, *Garden Maker*, 32.
22. Purifoy, *Garden Maker*, 11.
23. My journal February 17, 2023.
24. Nishi, *Zen Flowers*, 23.
25. Nishi, *Zen Flowers*, 64.
26. Nishi, *Zen Flowers*, 65.

> I delightfully noticed my first hydrangea bloom of the
> year in my garden. The idea that, in a few more weeks
> when many more blooms are out, they suggest the unity
> of all things within the universe is awesome. I have had
> hydrangea blooming for years in my garden and this is a
> real revelation—I will forever look at these blooms as the
> unity of everything in the universe.[27]

Costanzo wonders about the vital interdependency we have
with all living things to thrive and survive as she observes, listens,
and feels for her plants, perceiving the oneness of us saying, I can't
help but be in love and in joy here.[28] I journal after my walk in
the park: "The beautiful happy faces of all the wildflowers coming
into bloom, who seem delighted that I am noticing them, touches
my soul."[29]

Costanza senses joy is always present in her garden even when
little is blooming.[30] Chatto feels the joy from the daisy bush,[31] de-
scribing every time we walk past it a great gust of heliotrope scent
comes to meet us, interrupting whatever thoughts were running
in our minds.[32] Sharing her love of plants throughout her life with
all sorts of people, including children, has been a love affair for
Chatto.[33] When Chatto sees plants suffering from drought she
minimizes the effects of suffering by using mulches and manures,
believing that when your plants are happy, you are happy.[34] However, Chatto cautions on the use of water, our most precious com-
modity, and recommends reconsidering gardening practices given
the likelihood of hotter and drier summers to come in England.[35]

27. My journal May 5, 2023.

28. Costanzo, *Twelve Gifts*, 178.

29. My journal March 21, 2023.

30. Costanzo, *Twelve Gifts*, 197.

31. Botanical name *Olearia solandri*.

32. Chatto and Lloyd, *Dear Friend and Gardener*, 26.

33. Chatto and Lloyd, *Dear Friend and Gardener*, 11, 71.

34. Chatto and Lloyd, *Dear Friend and Gardener*, 16.

35. Chatto and Lloyd, *Dear Friend and Gardener*, 63.

Purifoy suspects heaven lies just behind the veil of this everyday world in her garden.[36] Roses are intoxicating, fascinating, and enchanting, casting a spell like no other flower.[37] Purifoy wants to travel back in time with the "Apothecary's Rose," its blood-red petals said to symbolize the Christian martyrs.[38] Abraham Lincoln said we can complain because rose bushes have thorns or rejoice because thorn bushes have roses.[39] Though the thorns are knife-sharp and the weeds are waging their wars, here is the promise that has been made to each of us: "May those who sow in tears reap with shouts of joy" (Ps 126:5 NRSV).[40]

Nothing expresses the emotional nakedness of the truth as the passion flower, writes Nishi, when its petals are wide open and its very heart is exposed, such poignant vulnerability deserves respect.[41] Looking into the heart of a flower and allowing what you find there to affect your inner feelings, those feelings will begin to multiply and soon your mind will be full of bright ideas.[42] I was inspired to journal:

> I began looking into the heart of daffodils—I can't find words for the amazing experience, beauty, and something profound and infinite. . . . It reminded me that I need to look into the depths of my own heart and acknowledge truthfully what I see there.[43]
>
> The lily petals in the vase on the table are just falling, so fascinating to hear their "thud" sound as they hit the table. They have been so angelic, so pure and white, looking into their very core, I noticed what seemed like tears on a few stamens earlier this week and wondered if they were weeping and, if so, what for.[44]

---

36. Purifoy, *Garden Maker*, 11.
37. Purifoy, *Garden Maker*, 29.
38. Purifoy, *Garden Maker*, 30.
39. Lincoln, *Collected Works*, 31.
40. Lincoln, *Collected Works*, 31
41. Nishi, *Zen Flowers*, 89.
42. Nishi, *Zen Flowers*, 92.
43. My journal March 20, 2023.
44. My journal May 20–23, 2023.

3.2. Beauty, Scent, and Color

The human soul is hungry for beauty, we seek it everywhere. When we experience the Beautiful, there is a sense of homecoming.[45] Nishi believes a single flower such as an allium says everything, liberating the beauty of the universe as it blooms.[46] The intoxicating scent of joewood draws people for a closer look, rewarding them with white, ivory, and creamy petals arranged in a star pattern.[47] Costanzo senses joewood is comfortable with itself, at peace with its slow pace of growth, its small size as well as its powerful beauty and its scent, saying, Be comfortable with yourself, don't compete, don't judge, just be.[48]

The beautyberry plant seemed nondescript in full flower.[49] In relooking at and appreciating her subtle beauty, learning that every part of the plant is useful for healing and nourishing humans and birds, Costanzo thanks her for teaching her not to jump to conclusions based on first impressions, remembering that everyone has hidden talents and beauty, which come at their own pace, in the right season, at their own time.[50]

In the wildflower garden, not only were they beautiful and fragrant, but there was a sense, a feeling from the plants of a congenial community in which all native plants relax in kinship and be themselves.[51] Costanzo found this to be soothing, nurturing, restful, and uplifting and felt enveloped by a soft yet joyful energy she imagined emanating from the cheerful plants.[52] It's as if authentic nature was encouraging her to be true to her real nature, not meeting others' expectations, accepting her innate worth and natural beauty as is, with self-compassion, self-love, and courage

45. John O'Donoghue quoted in Costanzo, *Twelve Gifts*, 36.
46. Nishi, *Zen Flowers*, 58.
47. Costanzo, *Twelve Gifts*, 106.
48. Costanzo, *Twelve Gifts*, 106.
49. Costanzo, *Twelve Gifts*, 60.
50. Costanzo, *Twelve Gifts*, 60.
51. Costanzo, *Twelve Gifts*, 67.
52. Costanzo, *Twelve Gifts*, 67.

to just be me.[53] This reminded me of my growth over the years and I journaled, "In the past, I often felt invisible, and I have awakened to accept that I am now blooming on my own path."[54]

In their letters to each other, Lloyd and Chatto describe various colors and scents: overwhelming vanilla scent from the vast white *Clematis montana*,[55] the yellow daffodils and pink mauve violets seem right together when they were starved of color for so long,[56] flowers attract them for their color and shapes.[57] Chatto is overjoyed with what she sees in her early morning walk in her garden and writes that you have to take time to stop and stare. The sunshine and shadows falling across the garden accentuate the dominant color, Chatto writes, and describes a thousand variations of luminous yellowy-green.[58]

Not all flowers have an uplifting scent. Lloyd describes the fetid smell of the dragon arums, *Dracunculus vulgaris*,[59] as more like rotten meat with a buzz of flies flying around the newly opened blooms.[60]

In August, Chatto notices that the colors are fading, observing that early morning or early evening is best to see the light shining through the transparent sickle-shaped pods of *Colutea arborescens*, or bladder senna, still carrying small, burnt-orange pea flowers on its tip shoots.[61] Lloyd, in his letter to Chatto, says everywhere is looking fresh and wonderful this September with color coming in fast all around, it's such an exciting time of year.[62]

53. Costanzo, *Twelve Gifts*, 67.

54. My journal May 17, 2023.

55. Chatto and Lloyd, *Dear Friend and Gardener*, 79.

56. Chatto and Lloyd, *Dear Friend and Gardener*, 44.

57. Chatto and Lloyd, *Dear Friend and Gardener*, 96.

58. Chatto and Lloyd, *Dear Friend and Gardener*, 57.

59. I use italics or plain text throughout my thesis to reflect how flowers are described in my data.

60. Chatto and Lloyd, *Dear Friend and Gardener*, 81.

61. Chatto and Lloyd, *Dear Friend and Gardener*, 238.

62. Chatto and Lloyd, *Dear Friend and Gardener*, 117.

Lloyd described today as being beautiful, made by finding the first two crocuses, not just there but open to the sun. He says he loves crocuses and tulips best of all, as they are the spring flowers that respond so gladly to encouragement from sunshine.[63] The color of the crocus is quite intense, purple rather than mauve, and with red stigmata—an exciting contrast.[64] Purifoy loves tulips and says they are pure color for our gardens.[65]

Chatto marvels every time she takes a deep breath at how fresh and intense the scent remains of a small packet of dried flowers, seeds, leaves, and tiny rosebuds from several years ago.[66] Chatto is completely unable to capture anything so fine and lasting.[67] When selecting new plants, she selects those with interesting foliage that are adapted to conditions, then pays attention to their flowers and more ephemeral color.[68] She is excited by chance seedlings that might inject color that she would not have thought of.[69]

3.3. Resilience

Flowers give you strength and inspiration.[70] From wildflowers pushing through cracks in sidewalks, Costanzo concluded that life has strength and determination; if plants can thrive in unfavorable conditions, I can too, she writes.[71]

Chatto describes how the rainstorms damaged the peonies, roses, bearded irises, and oriental poppies.[72] Lloyd, in his response, shares how the heavy August rains were ideal for flowers to bloom

63. Chatto and Lloyd, *Dear Friend and Gardener*, 16.

64. Chatto and Lloyd, *Dear Friend and Gardener*, 125.

65. Purifoy, *Garden Maker*, 189.

66. Chatto and Lloyd, *Dear Friend and Gardener*, 148.

67. Chatto and Lloyd, *Dear Friend and Gardener*, 148.

68. Chatto and Lloyd, *Dear Friend and Gardener*, 23.

69. Chatto and Lloyd, *Dear Friend and Gardener*, 148.

70. Nishi, *Zen Flowers*, 92.

71. Costanzo, *Twelve Gifts*, 24, 27.

72. Chatto and Lloyd, *Dear Friend and Gardener*, 223.

amid the parched countryside.[73] We have been through many storms, metaphorically speaking, of heartache, fear, grief, regrets, and anger and Costanzo notices how easy it is to turn and support each other during weather-related storms with courage, compassion, and unity.[74]

Costanzo wonders if a natural strengthening happens in the plants during a storm.[75] Maybe there is a plant form of faith that is part of their inherent will to survive.[76] This relates to post-traumatic growth that happens in humans after we have experienced trauma.[77] As some plants were destroyed by the storm and others survived, Costanzo feels grateful and blessed as it is part of how we maintain peace and well-being through life's gains and losses, noticing the good, finding the gifts, and recognizing the blessings.[78]

In spring, Costanzo notices new flower growth emerging all around her and their eagerness to grow with instinctive hope that they can have[79] a will to live with tenacious strength and determination.[80] Roses, phlox, and elderflower shrubs reach for the light, Purifoy observes, and are energized by it.[81] Costanzo contemplates "Light" and what Light is within us, concluding that the Light (Divine) in me sees and honors the Light in you.[82]

Chatto related the first crocuses opening wide as straight out of her idea of heaven.[83] She loves the crocuses for the way they respond when the weather relents.[84] I was thrilled to see the first flowers of spring and journaled:

73. Chatto and Lloyd, *Dear Friend and Gardener*, 259.
74. Costanzo, *Twelve Gifts*, 77.
75. Costanzo, *Twelve Gifts*, 78.
76. Costanzo, *Twelve Gifts*, 79.
77. Kiyimba, "Counsellors and Spiritual Directors," 138–56.
78. Costanzo, *Twelve Gifts*, 186.
79. Costanzo, *Twelve Gifts*, 195.
80. Costanzo, *Twelve Gifts*, 188.
81. Purifoy, *Garden Maker*, 47.
82. Costanzo, *Twelve Gifts*, 133.
83. Chatto and Lloyd, *Dear Friend and Gardener*, 31.
84. Chatto and Lloyd, *Dear Friend and Gardener*, 165.

> I saw beautiful crocuses in the park and the next day,
> when they were snow-covered, I wondered if they would
> survive. To my delight, they bounced back, reminding
> me that I should never underestimate mine or anyone's
> resilience—even these tiny, beautiful-colored flowers
> bounce back.[85]

Purifoy is full of hope and optimism in spring, wondering
what form of new-flowering life will grow.[86] She says that her dahl-
ias tell her every year that even when we stand at death's door, we
have not reached the end; everything, even death, is a return to
life.[87] Flowers grow because death can be fruitful and the resur-
rection is real.[88] Hope offers a fresh start and helps us find a space
through which we can move forward from a dispirited place, with
direction from inner wisdom, to a meaningful future as we adjust
to a new normal.[89]

Flower arranging soothes Nishi's tired spirit and, even when
not arranging flowers, she gets strength from just looking at
them.[90] When you see a single flower or an arrangement, Nishi
believes that you catch a frozen moment in its life, a symbol of
natural but fleeting perfection; then the flower continues the cycle
of life going back to the earth, nourishing and nurturing the next
generation of plants.[91] Flowers are an expression of implied perfection and part of an ongoing process of development, budding,
blooming, and finally withering.[92] The urge to thrive is innate in all
of us.[93] Sometimes to survive or thrive, we need to be "pruned" by

85. My journal March 8–13, 2023.
86. Purifoy, *Garden Maker*, 53.
87. Purifoy, *Garden Maker*, 184.
88. Purifoy, *Garden Maker*, 19.
89. Costanzo, *Twelve Gifts*, 195.
90. Nishi, *Zen Flowers*, 23.
91. Nishi, *Zen Flowers*, 22–23.
92. Nishi, *Zen Flowers*, 22.
93. Costanzo, *Twelve Gifts*, 189.

severing relationships, uprooting a fear, altering a limiting belief, or dropping an unhealthy habit, clearing the way for renewal.[94]

Daffodils, like roses, are a powerful symbol. Daffodils defined spring for Purifoy; lifting their golden trumpets, they sang spring.[95] Costanzo sees the urge, the will, the strength, and the courage to survive through the hundreds of new seedlings with instinctive hope that they can.[96] We know a flower only when we grow a flower and we know the flower deeply only when we grow a selection of that species—true knowing may take a lifetime.[97] If our lives are as ephemeral and fleeting as the life of a flower, then Purifoy sees every reason to spend her life growing and knowing all varieties of daffodils.[98]

3.4. Gratitude

Costanzo notes that today new flowers blossom and a gentle breeze comprise this magnificent moment for her,[99] paying homage where every plant is in full flower and the sun is always shining.[100] It is these moments that leave the deepest impression.[101] I journaled my delight with new blooms: "I was thrilled and so thankful to see lupines come into bloom, reminding me of happy childhood days."[102]

Growing flowers, including weeds, in planned and unplanned spaces is a living work of art, which Purifoy gives thanks for.[103] Costanzo has an abundance of appreciation for all things that sprout, grow, and bloom, having gratitude for how plants soothe, uplift, and feed us, enrich our minds, nourish our souls, help us

94. Costanzo, *Twelve Gifts*, 189.
95. Purifoy, *Garden Maker*, 56.
96. Costanzo, *Twelve Gifts*, 195.
97. Purifoy, *Garden Maker*, 56.
98. Purifoy, *Garden Maker*, 56.
99. Costanzo, *Twelve Gifts*, 100.
100. Purifoy, *Garden Maker*, 53.
101. Purifoy, *Garden Maker*, 53.
102. My journal May 22, 2023.
103. Purifoy, *Garden Maker*, 42.

breathe, have healing power, lead us toward understanding, and teach by example.[104]

Costanzo received twelve gifts from plants related to strength, beauty, courage, hope, compassion, joy, talent, imagination, reverence, wisdom, love, and faith through a collection of discoveries, healing perceptions, and aha experiences.[105] These gifts, she says, are a form of inner wealth which we all have and cultivating them can enrich every area of our lives.[106] Costanzo further describes these gifts as resources, capabilities, aptitudes, essences, powers, virtues, traits, and strengths.[107]

Costanzo recalls when, looking through her kitchen window as a child, her heart opened with gratitude and joy with the vibrant sight of morning glories blooming bright and blue, climbing a large trellis. Her love of them brought her to tears, teaching her that a shift in perspective can transform an experience.[108] For me, instead of just practically watering my flowers for survival as in previous years, I journal: "I am now deeply observant and compliment them on their beauty, color, hardiness, and determination to grow, all are magnificent including the pansies, lupines, angel flowers, and the calceolaria."[109]

Purifoy says we can grow roses as they ask to be seen—mysterious, yet if our heart longs for roses, plant roses even if their thorns draw blood when we tend them.[110] Like most plants, roses focus on growing roots first.[111] Chatto advises that light soil is ideal for growing roses.[112] Purifoy believes that seeds grow more than flowers as they grow a connection between her and her garden that

104. Costanzo, *Twelve Gifts*, 21.

105. Costanzo, *Twelve Gifts*, 21.

106. Costanzo, *Twelve Gifts*, 55.

107. Costanzo, *Twelve Gifts*, 54.

108. Costanzo, *Twelve Gifts*, 23.

109. My journal May 24, 2023.

110. Purifoy, *Garden Maker*, 30.

111. Purifoy, *Garden Maker*, 30.

112. Chatto and Lloyd, *Dear Friend and Gardener*, 223.

is deeper, richer, and more complete, rooting her there.[113] To be rooted is perhaps the most important need of the human soul.[114]

Nishi contemplates autumn being a time to reflect upon earthly existence as flowers change form and color, reminding us of our mortality. She says autumn is a melancholy but beautiful season.[115] When arranging flowers in recognition of all that fades away, Nishi gives silent thanks, for soon there will be another spring to enjoy.[116] Because flowers are never the same and our imaginations are unlimited there is endless scope when planning a floral composition.[117]

3.5. Awakening

Nishi believes that flowers inspire her and are stimuli to help her contemplate as she turns her thoughts inward away from daily distractions, emptying her mind and beginning her journey to her enlightenment.[118] Flowers, through their simple beauty and soothing qualities, can help people focus their mind to achieve a state of *mushin*, a state of total emptying of the mind.[119] By focusing her mind on flower arranging, Nishi achieves peace and harmony and discovers a whole new world of values.[120] The scattering of light and fragrance by the white or purple agapanthus diffuses their light and fragrance so they spread a sense of calm and inner peace.[121] Similar to Nishi, "I realize that transformation happens each time I joyfully arrange a bunch of flowers in a vase."[122]

113. Purifoy, *Garden Maker*, 66.

114. Costanzo, *Twelve Gifts*, 209.

115. Nishi, *Zen Flowers*, 103.

116. Nishi, *Zen Flowers*, 103, 82.

117. Nishi, *Zen Flowers*, 90.

118. Nishi, *Zen Flowers*, 27.

119. Nishi, *Zen Flowers*, 27.

120. Nishi, *Zen Flowers*, 6.

121. Nishi, *Zen Flowers*, 60.

122. My journal March 29, 2023.

When Costanzo sees someone's thorny hard exterior, she looks for their sparkle and flower and overlooks their thorns.[123] Nishi believes that by relooking at a flower that you know well, you can discover something new, indicating that something new and unexpected can be created by looking within.[124] This resonated with me as "I often make negative assumptions about a person or situation and, when challenged, I see things from a different perspective."[125]

When Costanzo looked with curiosity, fascination, and an open mind,[126] she saw the purple passionflower with its insides revealed, refusing to comply with the standard image of a flower, unequivocally proclaiming itself that it's good enough, it's okay to be different, odd, vulnerable, beautiful on all sides, and so are we.[127] Costanzo wishes we could all forgive ourselves for all the times we thought of ourselves as not good enough; we are enough.[128]

The Turk's cap mallow flower looks like it is continuously about to open, but it does not, which could seem that it never reaches its full potential. As Costanzo wondered if we ever fully open our minds or our hearts, this reminded her not to judge any person based on her expectations as she does not know their purpose and to accept everyone including ourselves as we are.[129] This prompted me to reflect after walking in my garden, "I am trying to be less judgmental and today I am accepting and treasuring all flowers, be they wildflowers such as daisies, dandelions, and poppies or cultivated flowers, for example, sweet william, foxgloves, roses, evening primrose, and campanula."[130]

123. Costanzo, *Twelve Gifts*, 35.

124. Nishi, *Zen Flowers*, 23.

125. My journal April 24, 2023.

126. Costanzo, *Twelve Gifts*, 119.

127. Costanzo, *Twelve Gifts*, 120.

128. Costanzo, *Twelve Gifts*, 162.

129. Costanzo, *Twelve Gifts*, 147–48.

130. My journal May 8, 2023.

Chatto described her enjoyment of each flower as she walked about her garden.[131] Too often we travel too fast, too busy to make time to stop and stare and sniff.[132] This triggered me, as I am frequently rushing here and there and not allowing myself to enjoy the here and now, to journal that "I am slowly getting better at slowing down and sniffing."[133]

Costanzo describes the flower, past-present-future,[134] which blooms for three days, changing from a vibrant periwinkle to a medium blue violet and then fading to white before falling to the ground.[135] She believes that we gain wisdom from the past when we look back with love and compassion, prepare for the future using imagination, and envision possibilities that bring out the best in us. We can accomplish these in the only time we have—here and now.[136] As I struggle with meditation, I journaled, "My biggest challenge is to live in the here and now,"[137] and "today, I allowed myself to be in the moment, smelling the beautiful heavenly fragrance from the choisya—a feast for my eyes and nose."[138]

4. Discussion of Findings

4.1. Emerging Themes Linked to Existing Literature

Writing became a way of contemplation, composed for the sheer joy of composition as this page became my "confidante of living thought."[139] I will discuss my findings against existing literature using the contemplative practices of *lectio* (reading), *meditatio* (interpreting), *oratio* (responding), and *contemplatio* (expressing

---

131. Chatto and Lloyd, *Dear Friend and Gardener*, 63.

132. Chatto and Lloyd, *Dear Friend and Gardener*, 253.

133. My journal May 5, 2023.

134. Botanical name is *Brunfelsia pauciflora*.

135. Costanzo, *Twelve Gifts*, 165.

136. Costanzo, *Twelve Gifts*, 167.

137. My journal May 9, 2023.

138. My journal May 19, 2023.

139. Versluis, *Awakening the Contemplative Spirit*, 55.

wisdom) that guided me into a subjective experience of wisdom and meaning.[140]

4.1.1. Love and Joy

Nhat Hanh compares love to compost that a gardener uses to grow flowers, nourishing new flowers of understanding and compassion in the garden of our hearts.[141] In Buddhism, there are four elements of true love: kindness, compassion, joy, and equanimity.[142] When you love without discrimination, you are practising true love and living in the most beautiful, peaceful, and joyous realm in the universe.[143] Masset loves growing flowers, believing it is because of the beauty of the bloom's shape, color, and texture and is now aware that there is a deep sense of peace and contentment, a feeling that envelops her, like an aura of gladness.[144]

Haviland-Jones et al. found when people received a bouquet of flowers, they smiled a true smile—a Duchenne smile that lights up the whole face, indicating genuine pleasure—and experienced a longer-lasting sense of good mood.[145] Hershey offers his observation of the air that is still full of hope and joy in the morning when the dew crystallizes on the ephemeral petals of the exquisite iris.[146]

4.1.2. Beauty, Scent, and Color

Yugen is the Japanese word for a profound mysterious sense of the beauty of the universe, the depth of this world as experienced through a cultivated imagination and an awareness of creation that triggers emotional responses too deep and powerful for

140. Keator, *Lectio Divina.*
141. Nhat Hanh, *Art of Living,* 135–36.
142. Nhat Hanh, *Teachings on Love,* 2.
143. Nhat Hanh, *Teachings on Love,* 2.
144. Masset, *Why We Garden,* 84–85.
145. Haviland-Jones et al., "Environmental Approach," 104–32.
146. Hershey, *Soul Gardening,* 36.

words.[147] Masset says beauty stops us in our tracks and produces a wonderful feeling of elation and enchantment, almost akin to a revelation, which takes us away from our chores and worries.[148] Stuart-Smith, who studied the relationship between gardening and mental health, says the experience of beauty in the fleeting moment leaves a trace in the mind that survives its passing moment.[149] Johnson feels the fleshy, apricot-white flowers of the "Treasure Trove " roses surging over a little bower of purple clematis as the most soul melting of all the flowers, believing this is Eden and words cannot express its beauty.[150]

Hershey is overjoyed with his garden visit.[151] He vividly outlines the color and smells of mock orange *Philadelphus* "Belle Etoile," bestowing its clean citrus perfume on any who pass by, magnetized by a mishmash of textures.[152] He elaborates on the narrow, lime-green leaves of *Penstemon glaber*, covered with a fluorescent cobalt flower, sharing space with the erect spires of a campanula extending its paper-thin, amethyst, bell-like flowers, and the needled pungency of rosemary.[153] In the book *Head Gardeners*, Mick describes the powerful experience of being enveloped in a corridor of light, vibrant colors, wanting to feel that the plants are embracing him.[154] Poppies have only one day to live but how imperially, how gorgeously they live it.[155] It is a reminder to me to live in the now and make the most of the beauty and life given to me. I, like Masset, marvel at poppies and their brilliant blooms and the beauty of serendipity.[156]

147. Costanzo, *Twelve Gifts*, 53.

148. Masset, *Why We Garden*, 16.

149. Stuart-Smith, *Well Gardened Mind*, 36.

150. Johnson, *Sitting in the Shade*, 35.

151. Hershey, *Soul Gardening*, 52.

152. Hershey, *Soul Gardening*, 52.

153. Hershey, *Soul Gardening*, 52.

154. Edwards, *Head Gardeners*, 80.

155. Purifoy, *Garden Maker*, 71.

156. Masset, *Why We Garden*, 48.

Kexiu et al. indicated green and green-white foliage plants enhanced relaxation and calmness in Japanese residents, while light green and green-yellow were the hues that Egyptian participants preferred for inducing calm.[157] By placing "greenness" at the heart of her thinking, Hildegard of Bingen recognized that people can only thrive when the natural world thrives.[158] A physician, Esther Stenberg explains that the photoreceptor gene that emerged first in evolutionary history is the one most sensitive to sunlight and the wavelengths of light reflected from green plants.[159] The amount of greenery we are exposed to is directly linked to how restorative it is.[160]

Aktekin et al. and Azeemi et al. suggest psychological responses vary with color: red is used to excite, activate, and arouse; blue to calm and relax; green to offer equilibrium; and yellow to uplift.[161] Hoyle et al. noted that the public views brightly colored flowers as extremely attractive and stimulating.[162] Neale et al. showed that warm flower colors altered heart rate variability and linked this to a restorative influence.[163]

Stuart-Smith describes the experience of losing herself when the deepest variegated blue of the tallest spiked delphinium commanded her attention, reminding her that she needs to stop and take heed of the beauty that is around her.[164] Johnson looks at a flower with a focused vision and delights in its texture, structure, the originality of its form, colors, and perhaps its scent,[165] which engages his senses and the intellect together, calling for patience in

---

157. Kexiu et al., "Foliage Colors Improve Relaxation."

158. Stuart-Smith, *Well Gardened Mind*, 29.

159. Stuart-Smith, *Well Gardened Mind*, 73.

160. Stuart-Smith, *Well Gardened Mind*, 73.

161. Aktekin and Simsek, "New Model for Chromotherapy," 154–56; Azeemi et al., "Mechanistic Basis of Chromotherapy," 217–22.

162. Hoyle et al., "All about the 'Wow Factor'?" 109–23.

163. Neale et al., "Color Aesthetics."

164. Neale et al., "Color Aesthetics."

165. Johnson, *Sitting in the Shade*, 209.

growing, nurturing, and waiting for maturity.[166] He describes the smell of the jasmine seedling that has appeared as Divine.[167]

Murray stops in her tracks and breathes in the richly perfumed, musky-smelling molecules wafting out from the peaches and cream-colored honeysuckle flowers.[168] When the hawthorn flowers are in bloom, Murray keeps her nose out for their rich aromas.[169] By taking time to smell the roses, Murray feels the textures, colors, patterns, scents, and sounds around us begin to reveal themselves.[170] The Mother believes that roses are the flowers to end all flowers; when a rose blossoms, it does so spontaneously for the joy of being beautiful, smelling sweet, expressing all its joy of living.[171]

The smell of the soaking garden, according to Johnson, is best of all as he wonders how rain releases so much scent into the air.[172] Pluviophile is a word for the love of rain and the scent of it.[173] The scent is derived from oil exuded by certain plants during dry periods and then absorbed into clay particles, which rain releases into the air along with another compound, geosmin: these are what we smell.[174] Costanzo delights in petrichor, the earthy smell after rainfall.[175] Mendelson says it makes one close one's eyes and inhale elemental breaths: water, decay, rust, life.[176]

166. Johnson, *Sitting in the Shade*, 209–10.

167. Johnson, *Sitting in the Shade*, 142.

168. Murray, *Wild Embrace*, 101.

169. Murray, *Wild Embrace*, 101.

170. Murray, *Wild Embrace*, 75.

171. The Mother, *Flowers and Their Spiritual Significance*, 8.

172. Johnson, *Sitting in the Shade*, 37.

173. Johnson, *Sitting in the Shade*, 38.

174. Johnson, *Sitting in the Shade*, 38.

175. Costanzo, *Twelve Gifts*, 55.

176. Mendelson, *Rhapsody in Green*, 69.

4.1.3. Resilience

Masset can't help but feel spiritually uplifted when the light, bees, and flowers conspire to produce a glorious atmosphere.[177] Wordsworth believed that a living relationship with nature is a source of strength that can help foster the healthy growth of the mind.[178] Hershey is convinced that by growing roses in intensive care units and displaying them at rose shows, many people who are now safely occupied with the care of the roses would be loose on the streets.[179]

In assessing yesterday's stormy rain damage, Hershey said the delphiniums and foxgloves are bent to breaking point, irreparable, fated to a spasmodic and flimsy posture.[180] One theory Hershey has is to let nature have its way as it cannot be regulated or controlled.[181] Stuart-Smith reflects on how her snowdrops are underground, naturally growing and replicating for most of the year, but for us humans, psychological repair does not come so naturally despite our mind's intrinsic drive toward growth and development.[182]

Rain falling is the sound of God washing his world, it's a cocoon soothing away all other sounds, and it's a luxury after a dry month.[183] However assiduously you water your plants, it's only drenching rain that brings such surges of growth.[184] This resonated with me as I journaled, "The red campions, foxgloves, lupines, and especially the roses have taken off with all of last week's rain."[185]

Redwood admires the plants we call "weeds," asking, Who are we to question the motives for their stubborn determination to insist on choosing their place to live despite our efforts to discourage

177. Masset, *Why We Garden*, 106.

178. Stuart-Smith, *Well Gardened Mind*, 14.

179. Hershey, *Soul Gardening*, 88.

180. Hershey, *Soul Gardening*, 97.

181. Hershey, *Soul Gardening*, 98.

182. Stuart-Smith, *Well Gardened Mind*, 23–24.

183. Stuart-Smith, *Well Gardened Mind*, 153.

184. Stuart-Smith, *Well Gardened Mind*, 217–18.

185. My journal May 14, 2023.

them?[186] I am constantly challenged by "weeds" that overgrow where I want other plants to flourish. I can learn from Anthony de Mello who shares the experience of the person who tried every method possible to get rid of the dandelions; the response he got when he finally wrote to the Department of Agriculture was, "We suggest you learn to love them."[187] In addition to learning to love the "weeds," I need to follow what Nhat Hanh says: "Attend to what causes my suffering and use them to create the most beautiful."[188] It is best not to impose our will upon nature but rather work with whatever is there and turn it toward balance, beauty, and harvest.[189]

Mendelson notes mid-autumn is a time of sorrow for fans of lupines and lobelias.[190] Everything is bending, browning, suffering from too little or too much weather, submitting to the fate that awaits us all: defoliation, discoloration, and death.[191]

Johnson, during the COVID-19 lockdown, reflected on all the time in the world we had to watch and enjoy nature's renewal as our plants were our companions, up close and personal.[192] He questioned the closing of plant nurseries to prevent the spread of COVID-19 during the height of the planting season, when plants were at the peak of their beauty and flower gardening is good for the nerves and for the soul.[193]

4.1.4. Gratitude

When persons are full of gratitude, all kinds of creativity come forth, imagination is freed, energy is restored, and generosity returns.[194] McClintock says gratitude immediately shifts one's atten-

186. Redwood, *Art of Mindful Gardening*, 54–55.

187. De Mello, *Awareness*, 58.

188. Nhat Hanh, *Together We Are One*, 15.

189. Versluis, *Awakening the Contemplative Spirit*, 83.

190. Mendelson, *Rhapsody in Green*, 148.

191. Mendelson, *Rhapsody in Green*, 148.

192. Johnson, *Sitting in the Shade*, 239.

193. Johnson, *Sitting in the Shade*, 241.

194. Fox, *Creation Spirituality*, 28.

tion away from the negative, away from the seemingly ordinary, and into the new, the good, and the beautiful.[195] Gratitude for the present moment and the fullness of life now, according to Tolle, is true prosperity.[196] Redwood believes autumn is a good time to give thanks for all that has grown both internally and externally,[197] recognizing that the roots of who we are lie in the darkness of the subconscious.[198]

Our emotions affect our bodies and the people around us, often fueling an emotional reaction from them, which in turn affects us.[199] When working with flowers, Redwood advises to try to see it as a dance of equals where both benefit, adopting an attitude of service to the greater good, and you will reap the rewards.[200] Hershey is initially disappointed when most of his lupines are nibbled by slugs, causing the plants to wilt and droop. His "pernickety cage" was rattled when he was surprised by and grateful for new flowers unexpectedly growing, such as the *Campanula lactiflora*, with its purple bellflowers pointing skyward.[201]

4.1.5. Awakening

Contemplating impermanence helps us touch freedom and happiness in the present moment, helping us see reality as it is, helping us embrace change, face our fears, and cherish what we have.[202] When we can see the impermanent nature of flowers, we can make a breakthrough into the heart of reality; a seed could never become a corn plant and the acorn couldn't become the oak tree, so impermanence is important for life as everything is possible.[203]

195. McClintock, "Opening the Heart," 21–22.

196. Tolle, *Power of Now*, 72.

197. Redwood, *Art of Mindful Gardening*, 98.

198. Redwood, *Art of Mindful Gardening*, 111.

199. Redwood, *Art of Mindful Gardening*, 133.

200. Redwood, *Art of Mindful Gardening*, 134.

201. Hershey, *Soul Gardening*, 103.

202. Nhat Hanh, *Art of Living*, 116.

203. Nhat Hanh, *Art of Living*, 116.

In resonating with another's spiritual experience this can be doubly self-implicating[204] as I experienced when I engaged my own spiritual experience and exposed my imagination and practice to significant influence from those I studied.

Enjoying plants is like music as both have been innate in us humans since the dawn of time.[205] Since I was a child, the scent of lilac has enchanted and stirred something within me. It stirred something deep within me that I could not name. Hershey also refers to childhood memories being stirred by the scent of lilac.[206] Murray recalls her first childhood memory in nature as being in awe of the blanket of primroses spreading about her.[207] She felt as if she had found a treasure hidden away in shady undergrowth where people did not dare to venture.[208] As an adult, Murray still finds the soft yellow perfection of swathes of primroses a magical and reassuring sight.[209] May Day brings memories back to Hershey when his mother sent him and his siblings to collect blooms from which they made May Day baskets. He can still picture daffodils, tulips, hyacinths, and cherry blossoms all crammed into the homemade baskets.[210]

Through the constant curiosity of the child, there is a dynamism of authenticity at work in our interiority, which is a dynamism of self-transcendence, attracting us to be the kind of person that keeps going until we have satisfied our seeking.[211] Opening our eyes to everyday experiences such as noticing pyramidal orchids with their intricately designed pink flowers cultivates our curiosity.[212] Being curious is one way we can deepen our connection to nature as it triggers our senses to produce a neurotransmitter

204. Frohlich, "Spirit, Spirituality, and Contemplative Method," 136.

205. Vincent, *Why Women Grow*, 162.

206. Hershey, *Soul Gardening*, 81.

207. Murray, *Wild Embrace*, 115.

208. Murray, *Wild Embrace*, 115.

209. Murray, *Wild Embrace*, 115.

210. Hershey, *Soul Gardening*, 81.

211. O'Sullivan, "Spiritual Capital," 45–53.

212. Murray, *Wild Embrace*, 79.

which hugely benefits our brain health.[213] The language of the soul includes descriptions of the body, intellect, memory, and will and the ability to engage in wonder, ability, and awe, which then calls for a response for care and action.[214]

Take a moment and look into a beautiful flower such as a daisy; by doing so, we can see that it is full of life containing soil, rain, and sunshine. It is also full of clouds, oceans, and minerals, even full of time and space, the entire cosmos present in this one flower.[215] If we take out one non-flower element, the flower would not be there.[216] Without the soil's nutrients, rain or sunshine, and other non-flower elements, the flower would die. Our observation tells us that the flower is full of the whole cosmos, it cannot exist by itself alone.[217] We too are full of so many things and yet empty of a separate self.[218] Like the daisy, we contain earth, water, air, sunlight and warmth, space and consciousness. The well-being of our body is not possible without the well-being of our planet; that is why, to protect the well-being of our body, we must protect the planet.[219]

When we are immersed in an enjoyable activity such as growing flowers, we experience flow. Flow is the experience of feeling at-oneness with the world, feeling one moment and action naturally flowing into the next.[220] The belief we can cultivate our soul or the self by gardening and pruning goes back to ancient times and is beginning to be applied to the brain in contemporary science.[221] The constant process of weeding, pruning, and fertilizing keeps the brain healthy at a cellular level.[222] Our emotional lives

---

213. Murray, *Wild Embrace*, 78.

214. Béres, *Language of the Soul*, 74.

215. Nhat Hanh, *Art of Living*, 12.

216. Nhat Hanh, *Art of Living*, 12.

217. Nhat Hanh, *Art of Living*, 12.

218. Nhat Hanh, *Art of Living*, 35.

219. Nhat Hanh, *Art of Living*, 35.

220. Masset, *Why We Garden*, 85; Mendelson, *Rhapsody in Green*, 74.

221. Stuart-Smith, *Well Gardened Mind*, 33.

222. Stuart-Smith, *Well Gardened Mind*, 35.

are complex and need constant tending and reworking, varying in form for each individual.[223]

By *being* in the morning, for example, noticing the flowers that grew overnight, Stuart-Smith says she can have the rest of her day for *doing*.[224] Redwood also writes about taking time to stand and stare at the buds breaking fresh, observing the rising tide of joy between the illusory boundary between our supposedly independent separate self and the environment, leaving us to feel more connected to and at one with nature.[225] Redwood recognizes flowers are just beings[226] and we need to remind ourselves that we are human *beings* and not human *doings*.[227]

Katagiri believes there is no way to discuss a beautiful blooming flower because it is beyond human speculation, concepts, or ideas; all you can do is pay attention to the reality of that flower as it really is.[228] When we find ourselves absorbed by the sweetness of ivy flowering in early winter, we may find that life is taking on a different hue.[229] To see this truth is to realize that the sacred and secular cannot be divided, with the most transcendent visions of spirituality shining through the here and now and how we live and love.[230]

Hershey explains how a single iris along the Colorado River arrested something rudimentary in him where he sat with only the glow of the flower, the warmth of the sun, the invigoration of the river's energy and strength with only mystery and awe . . . and peace.[231] Hershey sat for a spell in that presence and at home remembered that, Everywhere I am in Thy presence, knowing I hold

223. Stuart-Smith, *Well Gardened Mind*, 35.
224. Stuart-Smith, *Well Gardened Mind*, 278.
225. Redwood, *Art of Mindful Gardening*, 46.
226. Redwood, *Art of Mindful Gardening*, 63.
227. Redwood, *Art of Mindful Gardening*, 70.
228. Katagiri, *Each Moment Is the Universe*, 21.
229. Murray, *Wild Embrace*, 285.
230. Kornfield, *Path with Heart*, 57.
231. Hershey, *Soul Gardening*, 19.

something new and sacred in my heart.[232] Hershey then explains that he made a dramatic change in *his* life, quite by happenstance, when he planted a flower. He began to feel something come alive in his own skin as he saw the flower grow. He felt at home.[233] This is what is happening to me when I see the new blooms and growth in the garden. I journaled, "My inner excitement of seeing the foxglove bloom makes me feel that new life within me is blossoming."[234] Hershey came face to face with a part of himself that had been missing and he liked what he saw, the amazing inner sanctuary of the soul, a holy place, a Divine Center, a speaking Voice.[235] This delightfully and profoundly resonated with me, as it was the mystery of what is in the flower that deeply stirred me to do this research—I have now received a clear answer to my research question.[236] Hershey says our spiritual nature is enhanced when, for precious moments, we can shake that Voice and find ourselves knee-deep in the colors, smells, and emotions of the day; spirituality pushes us deeper and deeper into our existence.[237]

Gertrude Jekyll says nothing is better than to sit in front of plants, handle and look them over as carefully as possible, giving each plenty of time, and asking oneself and the plant, Why this? and Why that? and for one not to stir until one has found out why and how and what is it all about.[238] If you are one who sincerely seeks the truth, by living with a flower, you will find it.[239]

4.2. Expected and Unexpected Results

It was a personal joy to journey through the literature in search of what I was looking for and it was always an awakening when

232. Hershey, *Soul Gardening*, 19.
233. Hershey, *Soul Gardening*, 34.
234. My journal May 21, 2023.
235. Hershey, *Soul Gardening*, 34.
236. My journal May 23, 2023.
237. Hershey, *Soul Gardening*, 73–74.
238. Johnson, *Sitting in the Shade*, 67.
239. The Mother, *Flowers and Their Spiritual Significance*, 86.

something I read resonated with me. My biggest challenge was to keep focused on my research question as I read through the literature. It was academically challenging to compare lived experiences among the selected literature as few were in contrast to each other. Unexpectedly, I did not come across any current literature relating to the lived experience of Celtic spirituality of flowers or children's spiritual experience of flowers.

4.3. Limitations of My Research

Despite searching the SETU library, looking through many spiritual and flower-related journals and doing extensive internet searches, I found very limited research to address the lived experiences of my research question. When I did find some research, the sample sizes were very small and they were generally not location (urban, rural), age, well-being, nationality, or gender disaggregated.

I found lots of literature relating to the spirituality of gardening and to the spirituality of nature, including trees. As I was specifically looking at the spirituality of flowers, that literature did not answer my research question, though I was able to select some relevant data from books and articles on gardening and on nature.

4.4. Further Research: Contribution to Existing Research

I feel my research will add to existing knowledge on the spirituality of flowers, which is very scattered in various gardening and nature books. There is a huge scope for the spirituality of flowers to be presented on its own and for a great deal more research to be done on this as a distinguished topic separate from gardening.

This has the potential to benefit children and adults of all abilities and with special needs at the individual and the general public levels. This will allow opportunities to appreciate and, where possible, grow flowers of all shapes, colors, and scents to nourish their body, mind, and souls and ease frazzled nervous systems.[240] In addition, it will help contribute to the protection of Mother Earth.

5. Conclusion

My practice of authentic interiority, which is mystagogical, led me to the mysterious meaning about myself, others, and the wider world, which are the immanent experiences of the Transcendent.[241] The authenticity of the lived experience of my studied authors and myself of existing in our subjectivity in a state of dynamic orientation toward beauty, intelligibility, truth, goodness, and love[242] was evident throughout my research. By taking time to awaken my contemplative spirit and taking time to cultivate tranquillity and *being* in the moment, I feel I have progressed on *via positiva,*[243] an inner journey through a landscape of transfiguration. My research was transformative as not only did it answer my research question but it validated and amplified my own experiences of what flowers do for me.

Now more than ever, I realize how interdependent we humans are on all creation. Flowers are an essential part of creation. Appreciating them is a participation in a Divine-human transformation process expressed through our acknowledgment of the scent, color, shape, and any changes in these through our deep knowing that something sacred is within them.

Flowers are teachers bringing in wisdom and healing. As creation is always making new, enticing us to be fully present by taking precious moments to stand and smell the flowers, to re-"member" the whole of who we are as humans and care for Mother Earth, it enriches our souls. Rather than feeling so sad about the severity of the ecological loss, by appreciating flowers I am, in my small way, positively contributing to the world and cultivating a deeper love of nature which is joyful.

240. Murray, *Wild Embrace,* 239.

241. O'Sullivan, "Spiritual Practice of Authentic Interiority."

242. O'Sullivan, "Spiritual Capital and Authentic Subjectivity," 45–53.

243. Fox, *Creation Spirituality,* 20.

Appendix

Data Analysis

Words and Phrases	Cluster of Codes	Themes
I'm grateful for how plants soothe us and uplift us.	Grateful	Gratitude
I'm thankful that they feed our bodies.	Thankful	Gratitude
Enrich our minds and nourish our souls.	Soul nourishment	Mind
I have received a lot of lessons related to strength, beauty, courage, hope, compassion, joy, talent, imagination, reverence, wisdom, love, and faith. These gifts are a form of inner wealth which we all have and cultivating them can enrich every area of our lives.	Guidance Lessons Strength Beauty Courage Joy Love Inner wealth	Strength Beauty Joy Love Inner Wealth
Flowers are resources, capabilities, aptitudes, essences, powers, virtues, traits, and strengths.	Aptitudes Essences Strength	Strength
My heart opened with gratitude and joy.	Gratitude Joy	Gratitude Joy
If plants can thrive in unfavorable conditions, I can too.	Strength Resilience	Strength Resilience

Words and Phrases	Cluster of Codes	Themes
Look for their flower and overlook their thorns.	Mindful	Mindful
Talents and beauty come at their own pace, in the right season, in their own time.	Wisdom	Wisdom
Wildflower garden is soothing, nurturing, and felt enveloped by joyful energy emanating from the cheerful plants.	Nurturing Joy	Joy
Wise to brave those winds of heartache, fear, grief, regrets, and anger with courage, compassion, and unity.	Resilience Strength Compassion Unity	Resilience Strength
Today new flower blossoms comprise this magnificent moment for me.	Joy	Joy
Joewood's powerful beauty and scent.	Beauty Scent	Beauty Scent
Purple passion flower bare to the world with her insides revealed proclaiming that she is good enough, it is okay to be different. She is beautiful on all sides and so are we.	Acceptance Beautiful	Mindful Beauty
We are like the past-present-and-future which blooms only for three days but we, like the flowers, are always only in the now, it is here and now.	Being present Acceptance	Mindful
As I observe, listen, and feel, I perceive the Oneness of us—I can't help but be in love and joy here.	Love Joy Oneness	Love Joy
As some plants got destroyed by the storm and others survived, I feel grateful and blessed as it's part of how we maintain peace and well-being through life's gains and losses.	Strength Resilience Gratitude	Strength Resilience Gratitude
I sense joy even when little is blooming.	Joy	Joy

Words and Phrases	Cluster of Codes	Themes
Flower designing—reaching deep into my being takes me to a higher place, awakens my senses, and achieves peace and harmony.	Interiority Peace Awakening	Awakening Interiority
A single flower says everything; as it blooms it liberates the beauty of the universe.	Beauty	Beauty
By looking at a flower, it has a certain peace and tranquility that you can take into yourself, beginning to experience your true nature by reaching inward rather than looking outward.	Interiority True nature	Interiority
Flower arranging can help your contemplation and inspire you, turn your thoughts inward and begin your journey to enlightenment.	Contemplation Inspiration Enlightenment	Interiority
Flowers bloom everywhere . . . and in your heart.	Heart Love	Love
I *am in love* with flowers, with enchanting beauty and mysterious scents.	Love Beauty Scents	Love Beauty Scents
Flowers are rooted in love—growing flowers is a way of giving and receiving love.	Love Rooted	Love
Today has been beautiful by finding the first two crocuses.	Beautiful	Beauty
I love the crocus and tulips as they respond so gladly to encouragement from sunshine.	Love Encouragement	Love
The color of the crocus is quite intense, purple rather than mauve and red stigmata, an exciting contrast.	Color	Color
Olearia solandri is such a joy, a great gust of heliotrope scent comes to meet us.	Joy Scent	Joy Scent
I dropped to my knees to savor their scent.	Scent	Scent

Appendix

Words and Phrases	Cluster of Codes	Themes
You have to take time to stop and stare.	Interiority	Interiority
Flowers attract me for their color and shapes.	Color Shapes	Color
Description of flowers and their colors in all books.	Color	Color

Emerging Themes

Cluster of Codes	My Basis for Theme Development	Themes
Love and Joy	As both are closely linked, for ease of analysis, I grouped them.	Love and Joy
Interiority, Mindful, Oneness, *Being present*, Enrich our minds, Lessons, Wisdom	As these all relate to our spiritual awakening, I feel the best word to capture these codes is Awakening.	Awakening
Beauty, Scent, and Color	These describe aspects of flowers that awakened my and the author's reviewed senses.	Beauty, Scent, and Color
Strength and Resilience	I have opted for Resilience which includes Strength, as I feel it better describes the flowers' and humans' ability to withstand challenges.	Resilience
Grateful, Thankful, Gratitude	I feel the word Gratitude is inclusive of the other two words.	Gratitude

Bibliography

Ahmad, Iqbal, et al., eds. *Modern Phytomedicine: Turning Medicinal Plants into Drugs.* Wiley-VCH, 2006. https://onlinelibrary.wiley.com/doi/book/10.1002/9783527609987.

Aktekin, Deniz Basbinar, and Yusuf Simsek. "A New Model for Chromotherapy Application." *Color Research and Application* 37:2 (April 2012) 154–56. https://doi.org/10.1002/col.20658.

Anderson, Rosemarie. "Transformative Research Methods: Research to Nourish the Spirit." *Journal for the Study of Spirituality* 10:1 (2020) 95–103. https://doi.org/10.1080/20440243.2020.1726056.

Anderson, Rosemarie, and William Braud. *Transforming Self and Others through Research: Transpersonal Research Methods and Skills for the Human Sciences and Humanities.* Albany: State University of New York Press, 2011.

Azeemi, Samina T. Yousuf, et al. "The Mechanistic Basis of Chromotherapy: Current Knowledge and Future Perspectives." *Complementary Therapies in Medicine* 46 (October 2019) 217–22. https://doi.org/10.1016/j.ctim.2019.08.025.

Bailey, Martin. *The Sunflowers Are Mine: The Story of Van Gogh's Masterpiece.* London: Quarto, 2019.

Beevers, John. *St. Therese the Little Flower: The Making of a Saint.* Gastonia, NC: TAN Books, 2009.

Béres, Laura. *The Language of the Soul in Narrative Therapy: Spirituality in Clinical Theory and Practice.* New York: Routledge, 2022.

Berger, Roni. "Now I See It, Now I Don't: Researcher's Position and Reflexivity in Qualitative Research." *Qualitative Research* 15:2 (2015) 219–34.

Berry, Thomas. "Contemporary Spirituality: The Journey of the Human Community." *Crosscurrents* 24:2/3 (Summer/Fall 1974).

———. *The Dream of the Earth.* Berkeley: Counterpoint, 2015.

Bibliography

Braud, William, and Rosemarie Anderson. *Transpersonal Research Methods for the Social Sciences: Honouring Human Experience.* London: Sage Publications, 1994.

Braun, Virginia, and Victoria Clarke. *Thematic Analysis: A Practical Guide.* London: Sage Publications, 2022.

Carson, Rachel. *Silent Spring.* Boston: Houghton Mifflin, 1962.

Chalmin-Pui, Lauriane Suyin, et al. "Why Garden?—Attitudes and the Perceived Health Benefits of Home Gardening." *Cities* 112 (May 2021). https://doi.org/10.1016/j.cities.2021.103118.

Chan, Thomas Y. K. "Aconite Poisoning." *Clinical Toxicology* 47:4 (2009) 279–85. https://doi.org/10.1080/15563650902904407.

Chatto, Beth, and Christopher Lloyd. *Dear Friend and Gardener: Letters on Life and Gardening.* London: Quarto, 2021.

Chemer, Anthony. *Radical Embodied Cognitive Science.* Cambridge: MIT Press, 2011.

Chopra, Deepak. *The Seven Spiritual Laws of Success.* London: Bantam, 2014.

Christie, Douglas E. *The Insurmountable Darkness of Love: Mysticism, Loss, and the Common Life.* Oxford: Oxford University Press, 2021.

Costanzo, Charlene. *The Twelve Gifts from the Garden: Life Lessons for Peace and Well-Being.* Coral Gables, FL: Mango, 2020.

Critchlow, Keith. *The Hidden Geometry of Flowers: Living Rhythms.* Edinburgh: Floris, 2011.

De Mello, Anthony. *Awareness.* New York: Doubleday, 1990.

Dobbs, Liz. *The Secret Language of Flowers.* London: Penguin Random House, 2022.

Edwards, Ambra. *Head Gardeners.* London: Pimpernel Press, 2021.

Evancic, Monique. "Unexpected Meanings of Flowers Revealed | Monique Evancic | TEDxBoise." TEDx Talks, YouTube, May 31, 2019. https://www.youtube.com/watch?v=eoQx6vigMBk.

Fenton, Will. "35 Best Songs about Flowers of All Time." Midder, Dec. 6, 2023. https://middermusic.com/songs-about-flowers/.

Ferguson, Diana. *Old Wives Lore for Gardeners.* London: Michael O'Mara Books, 2021.

"Flowers in Cinema." Something Curated, June 14, 2021. https://somethingcurated.com/2021/06/14/flowers-in-cinema/.

Fox, Matthew. *Creation Spirituality: Liberating Gifts for the Peoples of the Earth.* New York: HarperCollins, 1991.

Francis, Pope. *Praise Be to You—Laudato Si': On Care for Our Common Home.* San Francisco: Ignatius, 2015.

Frohlich, Mary. "Contemplative Method and the Spiritual Core of Higher Education." In *The Soul of Higher Education: Contemplative Pedagogy, Research, and Institutional Life for the Twenty-First Century,* edited by Margaret Benefiel and Bo Karen Lee, 13–30. Charlotte: Information Age, 2019.

———. "Critical Interiority." *Spiritus* 7 (2007) 77–81.

Bibliography

———. "Spirit, Spirituality, and Contemplative Method." *Teologia Spirituale* 12:2 (2019) 133–36.

Griffiths, Bede. *The Cosmic Revelation: The Hindu Way to God*. London: Collins, 1983.

Guthrie, Stewart. *Faces in the Church: A New Theory of Religion*. London: Oxford University Press, 1993.

Hansen, Gail, and Erin Alvarez. "Color in the Landscape: Finding Inspiration for a Color Theme." Environmental Horticulture, UF/IFAS Extension, May 9, 2019. https://edis.ifas.ufl.edu/publication/EP425.

Haviland-Jones, Jeannette, et al. "An Environmental Approach to Positive Emotion: Flowers." *Evolutionary Psychology* 3:1 (2005). https://doi.org/10.1177/147470490500300109.

Heilmeyer, Marina. *The Language of Flowers: Symbols and Myths*. New York: Prestel, 2001.

Hershey, Terry. *Soul Gardening: Cultivating the Good Life*. Minneapolis: Monarch, 2002.

Hollick, Malcolm, and Christine Connelly. *Hope for Humanity: How Understanding and Healing Trauma Could Solve the Planetary Crisis*. Ropley, UK: O Books, 2010.

Hoyle, Helen, et al. "All about the 'Wow Factor'? The Relationships between Aesthetics, Restorative Effect, and Perceived Biodiversity in Designed Urban Planting." *Landscape and Urban Planning* 164 (August 2017) 109–23. https://doi.org/10.1016/j.landurbplan.2017.03.011.

Huss, Ephrat, et al. "Humans' Relationship to Flowers as an Example of the Multiple Components of Embodied Aesthetics." *Behavioral Sciences* 8:3 (March 2018) 32. https://doi.org/10.3390/bs8030032.

Johnson, Hugh. *Sitting in the Shade: A Decade of My Garden Diary*. London: Mitchell Beazley, 2021.

Jung, Jihye, et al. "Beyond Chemical Triggers: Evidence for Sound-Evoked Physiological Reactions in Plants." *Frontiers in Plant Science* 9 (January 2018). https://doi.org/10.3389/fpls.2018.00025.

Katagiri, Dainin. *Each Moment Is the Universe: Zen and the Way of Being Time*. Boston: Shambhala, 2009.

Keator, Mary. *Lectio Divina as Contemplative Pedagogy: Re-Appropriating Monastic Practice for the Humanities*. New York: Routledge, 2019.

Kerr, Jessica. *Shakespeare's Flowers*. London: Book Club Associates, 1970.

Kexiu, Liu, et al. "Foliage Colors Improve Relaxation and Emotional Status of University Students from Different Countries." *Heliyon* 7:1 (January 2021). https://doi.org/10.1016/j.heliyon.2021.e06131.

Khait, Itzhak, et al. "Sounds Emitted by Plants Under Stress Are Airborne and Informative." *Cell* 186:7 (March 30, 2023). https://doi.org/10.1016/j.cell.2023.03.009.

Khan, Aisha. *Callaloo Nation: Metaphors of Race and Religious Identity among South Asians in Trinidad*. Durham, NC: Duke University Press, 2004.

Kiyimba, Nikki. "What Counsellors and Spiritual Directors Can Learn from Each Other." In *Ethical Practice, Training, and Supervision*, edited by Peter Madsen Gubi, 138–56. London: Jessica Kingsley, 2017.

Klesius, Michael. "The Big Bloom: How Flowering Plants Changed the World." *National Geographic*, July 2002, 102–21.

Kornfield, Jack. *A Path with Heart*. New York: Bantam, 1993.

Kramer, Dietmar. *New Bach Flower Therapies: Healing the Emotional and Spiritual Causes of Illness*. Rochester, VT: Healing Arts, 1995.

Kumar, Satish. *Soil, Soul, Society: A New Trinity for Our Time*. Lewes, UK: Leaping Hare, 2013.

Lincoln, Abraham. *Collected Works of Abraham Lincoln*. Edited by Roy P. Basler. 8 vols. Cabin John, MD: Wildside Press, 2008.

Lonergan, Bernard J. F. *Method in Theology*. Toronto: Toronto University Press, 1990.

———. *Phenomenology and Logic: The Boston College Lectures on Mathematical Logic and Existentialism*. Edited by Philip McShane. Vol. 18 of *Collected Works of Bernard Lonergan*. Toronto: University of Toronto Press, 2018.

Masset, Claire. *Why We Garden: The Art, Science, Philosophy and Joy of Gardening*. London: Batsford, 2023.

McAloon, Francis X. "Reading for Transformation through the Poetry of Gerard Manley Hopkins." *Spiritus* 8:2 (Fall 2008) 182–201. https://doi.org/10.1353/scs.0.0035.

McClintock, Clayton H. "Opening the Heart: A Spirituality of Gratitude." *Spirituality in Clinical Practice* 2:1 (March 2015) 21–22. https://doi.org/10.1037/scp0000060.

Mendelson, Charlotte. *Rhapsody in Green*. London: Kyle, 2016.

Miller, Lewis. "The Power of Flowers | Lewis Miller | TEDxCharlottesville." TEDx Talks, YouTube, Feb. 7, 2020. https://www.youtube.com/watch?v=JCVUyeHD2lQ.

Morales, Fátima, et al. "Medicinal Plants Used in Traditional Herbal Medicine in the Province of Chimborazo, Ecuador." *African Journal of Traditional, Complementary and Alternative Medicines* 14:1 (2017) 10–15. https://doi.org/10.21010/ajtcam.v14i1.2.

The Mother. *Flowers and Their Spiritual Significance*. Pondicherry, India: Sri Aurobindo Society, 2012.

Murray, Anja. *Wild Embrace: Connecting to the Wonder of Ireland's Natural World*. Dublin: Hachette Ireland, 2023.

Nadot, Sophie, and Laetitia Carrive. "The Colourful Life of Flowers." *Botany Letters* 168:1 (2021) 120–30. https://doi.org/10.1080/23818107.2020.1839789.

Naydler, Jeremy. *Gardening as a Sacred Art*. Edinburgh: Floris, 2011.

Neale, Chris, et al. "Color Aesthetics: A Transatlantic Comparison of Psychological and Physiological Impacts of Warm and Cool Colors in Garden Landscapes." *Wellbeing, Space and Society* 2 (2021). https://doi.org/10.1016/j.wss.2021.100038.

Newell, John Philip. *Sacred Earth Sacred Soul: A Celtic Guide to Listening to Our Souls and Saving the World*. Dublin: HarperCollins, 2021.

Nhat Hanh, Thich. *The Art of Living*. London: Penguin, 2017.

———. *Together We Are One: Honoring Our Diversity, Celebrating Our Connection*. Berkeley: Parallax, 2010.

———. *You Are Here*. Boston: Shambhala, 2009.

NicUaithuas, Máire Éibhlís. "Spirituality, Social Concern and Gender." Module for the MA in Applied Spirituality, SETU Waterford, 2022–2023.

Nishi, Harumi. *Zen Flowers: Contemplation through Creativity*. Montenegro: Aquamarine, 2001.

O'Callaghan, Casey. "Object Perception: Vision and Audition." *Philosophy Compass* 3:4 (July 2008) 803–29. https://doi.org/10.1111/j.1747-9991.2008.00145.x.

O'Donoghue, John. *Divine Beauty: The Invisible Embrace*. London: Bantam, 2004.

Oliver, Mary. *The Blue Iris*. Boston: Beacon, 2006.

Ó Murchú, Diarmuid. *Reclaiming Spirituality*. Dublin: Gill & Macmillan, 1997.

O'Sullivan, Michael. "Authenticity as a Spirituality Process and Practice." Module for the MA in Applied Spirituality, SETU Waterford, 2022–2023.

———. "Authentic Subjectivity as a Methodology for Studying Spirituality." *Teologia Spirituale* 12:2 (2019) 277.

———. "Reflexive and Transformative Subjectivity: Authentic Spirituality and a Journey with Incest." In *Sources of Transformation: Revitalizing Christian Spirituality*, edited by Edward Howells and Peter Tyler, 173–82. London: Continuum, 2010.

———. "Spiritual Capital and Authentic Subjectivity." In *Sacrality and Materiality*, edited by Rebecca Giselbrecht and Ralph Kunz, 45–53. Gottingen: Vandenheck and Ruprecht, 2015.

———. "The Spiritual Practice of Authentic Interiority." Paper presented at the Cave of the Heart: Contemplation, Mindfulness, and Social Renewal Conference, St. Mary's University College, London, 30 June 2012.

Pallasdowney, Rhonda M. *Voices of Flowers: Use the Natural Wisdom of Plants and Flowers for Health*. Newburyport, MA: Weiser, 2006.

Palmer, Parker J. *Let Your Life Speak: Listening for the Voice of Vocation*. San Francisco: Jossey-Bass, 2000.

Proust, Milli. *From Seed to Bloom: A Year of Growing and Designing with Seasonal Flowers*. London: Quadrille, 2022.

Purifoy, Christie. *Garden Maker: Growing a Life of Beauty and Wonder with Flowers*. Eugene, OR: Harvest House, 2022.

Redwood, Ark. *The Art of Mindful Gardening: Sowing the Seeds of Meditation*. London: Leaping Hare, 2018.

Robinson, William. *The English Flower Garden: Style, Position, and Arrangement*. New York: Cambridge University Press, 2011.

Sartiliot, Claudette. *Herbarium Verbarium: The Discourse of Flowers*. Lincoln: University of Nebraska Press, 1993.

Bibliography

Schneiders, Sandra. "Approaches to the Study of Christian Spirituality." In *The Blackwell Companion to the Study of Christian Spirituality*, edited by Arthur Holder, 15–34. Malden, MA: Wiley-Blackwell, 2005.

———. *The Revelatory Text: Interpreting the New Testament as Sacred Text*. Collegeville, PA: Liturgical Press, 1999.

Shapiro, Lawrence. *Handbook of Embodied Cognition*. London: Routledge, 2014.

Sheldrake, Philip. *Spirituality: A Very Short Introduction*. Oxford: Oxford University Press, 2012.

Solecki, Ralph S. *Shanidar: The First Flower People*. New York: Knopf, 1971.

Stenta, N. "From Other Lands: The Use of Flowers in the Spirit of the Liturgy." *Orate Fratres* 4 (1930) 462–69.

Strehlow, Wighard, and Gottfried Hertzka. *Hildegard of Bingen's Medicine*. Sante Fe: Bear & Company, 1988.

Stuart-Smith, Sue. *The Well Gardened Mind: Rediscovering Nature in the Modern World*. London: HarperCollins, 2021.

Swimme, Brian, and Mary Evelyn Tucker. *Journey of the Universe*. New Haven: Yale University Press, 2011.

Taylor, Edward, et al. *The Handbook of Transformative Learning: Theory, Research, and Practice*. San Francisco: John Wiley & Sons, 2012.

Teilhard de Chardin, Pierre. *The Human Phenomenon*. Edited by Sarah Appleton-Weber. Brighton UK: Sussex Academic Press, 2003.

Thompson, April. "Gardening as Spiritual Practice: Cycles of Growth Cultivate Our Divinity." Natural Awakenings, Feb. 28, 2014. https://www.naturalawakenings.com/2014/02/28/272237/gardening-as-spiritual-practice-cycles-of-growth-cultivate-our-divinity.

Tolle, Eckhart. *A New Earth: Create a Better Life*. London: Penguin, 2018.

———. *The Power of Now*. London: Hodder and Stoughton, 2005.

Torralba, Antonio, and Aude Oliva. "Statistics of Natural Image Categories." *Network* 14:3 (July 2003) 391–412. https://doi.org/10.1088/0954-898X_14_3_302.

Ullman, Shimon, et al. "Visual Features of Intermediate Complexity and Their Use in Classification." *Nature Neuroscience* 5 (July 2002) 682–727. https://doi.org/10.1038/nn870.

Varela, Francisco J., et al. *The Embodied Mind: Cognitive Science and Human Experience*. Cambridge, MA: MIT Press, 1991.

Varela, Francisco J., and Jonathan Shear. "First-Person Methodologies: What, Why, How?" *Journal of Consciousness Studies* 6, vol. 2–3 (1999) 10.

Versluis, Arthur. *Awakening the Contemplative Spirit*. St. Paul: New Grail, 2004.

Vincent, Alice. *Why Women Grow: Stories of Soil, Sisterhood and Survival*. Edinburgh: Canongate, 2023.

Vinje, Eric. "The Spirit of Gardening." Planet Natural Research Center, updated Feb. 26, 2020. https://www.planetnatural.com/spiritual-gardening/.

Waaijman, Kees. *Forms, Foundations, Methods*. Leuven: Peeters, 2002.

Bibliography

Wall, Vicky. *Auro Soma: Self Discovery through Color*. Rochester, NY: Inner Traditions Bear and Company, 2005.

Whitmore, John. *Coaching for Performance*. London: Nicholas Brealey, 2017.

Wilson, Kendra. *Garden for the Senses*. London: Penguin Random House, 2022.

Woodhouse, Patrick. *Etty Hillesum: A Life Transformed*. London: Continuum, 2009.

Wordsworth, William. *The Book of Flowers: Wordsworth's Poetry on Flowers*. Redditch, UK: Ragged Hand-Read & Co., 2020.

Worwood, Valerie Ann. *The Fragrant Mind*. London: Transworld Ltd, 1997.

Zhang, An Lan. *Flowers in Chinese Culture: Folklore, Poetry, Religion*. St. Petersburg, FL: Three Pines, 2015.

Zhang, Liwen, et al. "Flowers—Sunshine for the Soul! How Does Floral Colour Influence Preference, Feelings of Relaxation and Positive Up-Lift?" *Urban Forestry & Urban Greening* 79 (January 2023). https://doi.org/10.1016/j.ufug.2022.127795.

Zheng, Jingyun, et al. "An Update on the Health Benefits Promoted by Edible Flowers and Involved Mechanisms." *Food Chemistry* 340 (March 15, 2021). https://doi.org/10.1016/j.foodchem.2020.127940.